AD HOC, AD LIB, AD NAUSEAM

So You Think
You Don't Speak
Latin?

JOHN PARKER

By the same author:

Crossnumbers

Reading Latin Epitaphs

The Platonic Solids

Keskowsow (Conversations in Cornish)

Contents

Introduction

Wherever we go in our journey through the intricate paths of the English language, we cannot escape the influence of Latin. Latin has long been a linguistic meadow from which innovative writers throughout the centuries have culled the blossoms they needed to put their thoughts into words, and the chronology of their inventions and borrowings is a fascinating study. Latin is commonly regarded as a dead language, but words and phrases live on.

This book has three main purposes. *Imprimis*, it celebrates Latin as a beautiful language, displaying for the pleasure of the present reader some of its multitude of treasures. *Item*, it tries to help readers divine the meaning of some of the Latin phrases they may encounter. *Item*, it seeks to encourage readers to risk adding Latin phrases to their vocabulary.

There are those who advocate using only English words and phrases in English speech and writing, but I believe these people have no ear for the music of language. English owes much of its colour to the occasional appearance of a foreign word or phrase, such as 'tête-à-tête' or *schadenfreude* or *in situ*, et cetera. Lately the use of Latin has been discouraged in English courts of law; but what harm is there in using terms such as 'in camera' or *sine die* or *pro bono*, phrases with no succinct English equivalent? Without the power to draw on foreign languages to express what are often foreign ideas and concepts, English becomes clumsy and loses force. In the opinion of Dr Samuel Johnson, 'a scripture expression may be used like a highly classical phrase to produce an instantaneous strong impression'. (James Boswell, *The Life of Samuel Johnson, LL.D.*)

Most of the words and short phrases which appear in this book have been passed down orally from one generation to the next and have been absorbed into the mother tongue. Such phrases as 'et cetera', 'per se', 'in flagrante', 'non sequitur' and 'quid pro quo' can be counted as being quasi-English by virtue of their frequent and long-standing use.

Even though dead, Latin still seems to have a certain cachet in some quarters. The names chosen by pop groups such as Status Quo and Procul Harum exemplify this. More sober institutions use Latin in the same way: a magazine described as 'the thinker's garden quarterly' is called *Hortus*, which is 'garden' in Latin.

It has frequently been pointed out that a great part of the English language is anyway no more than thinly disguised Latin. To a Roman of 100 BC the words 'intricate' and 'influence' would have seemed curiously familiar, reminding him of *in-tricae* and *in-fluere*. He might study the word 'ubiquitous' and wonder perhaps if it had any connection with *ubique*. He might see in 'circumvent' a curtailment of *circumventus*, and so ad infinitum (or very nearly so).

A further point which has been made is this. Many words of Latin origin were brought into Middle

English to dignify the vocabulary of philosophy or of the natural sciences, to fill gaps where there was no suitable English word available, or to supply single words in place of English phrases – 'dignify' in place of 'make worthy', 'vocabulary' in place of 'word list'. But when we use a word like 'intervene' as a more elegant alternative to 'come between', we should realise that to our Ancient Roman the word *intervenire* meant literally nothing less than 'come between', and that to *intervenire* in a quarrel meant putting oneself bodily between the two who were fighting it out. When the Romans wanted words to supply gaps in their own philosophical lexicon, they borrowed from Greek.

A book of this nature can never be finished. Any author, if his reading continues to be sufficiently wide, will always be coming across new Latin phrases which deserve inclusion, or fresh examples of the use of existing phrases.

I hope this book, incomplete though it may be, will encourage readers to continue to use Latin phrases whenever they are appropriate and to add a few new ones to their arsenal.

John Parker

Pronunciation

Until about 1920, Latin was pronounced in Britain as though it were English. The old pronunciation still persists in such phrases as 'et cetera', 'prima facie', *'sub judice'* and 'vice versa'. Then scholars decided that if the language was to be taught at all in schools and colleges, it should be spoken as the Romans spoke it (according to the scholars' conjecture about Roman pronunciation, there being little if any record of how the average Roman actually spoke); and from that time forth uncertainty reigned, and spoken Latin in Britain entered a decline.

The Romans used the letter 'V' for writing both 'V' and 'U': what they pronounced as 'unus' they wrote as 'vnvs', and the letter 'V' in Latin was pronounced either as 'U' or as 'W', but never as 'V'. Likewise where the Romans used 'I' at the start of a word, followed by another vowel, as in 'ianitor', we tend to use 'J' ('janitor'); however, they pronounced the initial 'I' not as 'J' but as 'Y'. They pronounced 'C' as 'K' and not as 'S' or 'CH', and 'G' was hard as in 'girl' and never soft as in 'gentle'. Their vowel sounds were much the same as they still are in Rome nowadays, so if we use present-day Italian values for the vowel sounds we shall not go far wrong. So the word 'vice' should strictly speaking be pronounced as 'wee-kay' and 'judice' as 'you-dee-kay'. It is clear why Latin scholars became torn between tradition and their own conscience, and grew shy of using Latin in everyday speech, other than those words and phrases such as 'verbatim', 'ex officio', 'versus', 'Julius Caesar' et al., which had become anglicised beyond redemption.

How should we pronounce Latin words when they occur in English? Most words and phrases present no problem. There is a limit to the number of different ways in which we can say *ipsissima verba* or *in articulo mortis*, and there is everything to be said for sticking to the traditional English pronunciation of most phrases. Many people, perhaps through having learned a little Latin at school, tend to pronounce *Te Deum* as 'tay day-um' rather than as 'tee dee-um' which was the old English way. 'Deity' was for centuries pronounced 'dee-ity', but is now often pronounced 'day-ity' . Those who want to use the Received Latin pronunciation are free to do so, and can find it explained in any grammar book. Others might prefer to adopt the ecclesiastical pronunciation. One's chosen pronunciation can be tempered by listening to Latin as spoken by the presenters of radio music programmes, who are frequently called on to announce the Latin titles of pieces of sacred music.

It is a matter of personal preference.

Notes

A few Latin words, sometimes abbreviated, are used as instructions in this book. Each is explained as a separate entry in the book, but here is a list for easy reference.

cf. (confer)	compare
infra	below
passim	throughout
q.v. (quod vide)	which see
supra	above
vide	see

This selection contains single words or short phrases in Latin which enrich the vocabulary of English. It also contains quotations mostly from the classical Latin writers, together with a number of extracts from the Vulgate Bible, with corresponding English verses from the Authorised Version. In addition, there are extracts from the Ordinary of the Mass in the Roman Catholic Church, with their new English replacements. These last will be referred to simply as being extracts from 'The Mass'. The Vulgate translation of the Bible was made in the fourth century by St Jerome, was subsequently twice revised, and was the version of the Bible used in the Roman Catholic Church.

Ab initio

From the beginning, at the outset

'I tell you, Gillett, if the Romans had dealt faithfully with the Celt, *ab initio*, this – this would never have happened.'

Rudyard Kipling, 'The Propagation of Knowledge'

In 'Poor Koko', John Fowles asks if the poverty of the phrase 'to tell it as it really is' did not '*ab initio* castrate the wish it implied'.

In science, *ab initio* is used to mean 'from first principles'. For example, a particular system may be advertised to those in the know as consisting of '*ab initio* programs for molecular electronic structure calculations'.

Ab origine

From the beginning, from the source

Aboriginal inhabitants of a country, or *aborigines*, have evolved there, or at least have been minding their own business there for a long time, in contrast to later immigrants.

'These ladies sat side by side with young females destined to be *demoiselles de magazins*, and with some Flamandes, genuine aborigines of the country.'

Charlotte Brontë, *The Professor*

Ab urbe condita (AUC)
From the building of the city (Rome)

Every civilisation uses a calendar in which years are numbered from some landmark event in the past. For the Jews it is the Creation, for the Muslims it is the Hegira, for the Western nations it is the birth of Christ. For the Romans it was the year in which Rome was built. All happenings in Roman history were dated from this point, which we know as 753 BC but which to the Romans was their year dot or zero. An alternative form is *Anno urbis conditae* ('In the year from the building of the city').

Frank Morley, in *The Great North Road*, transfers the phrase from Rome to London: '… the north front of the Wall… was now disclosed… as it was *ab urbe condita.*'

In A. S. Byatt's *Angels and Insects*, Natty Crompton, speaking of the Blood-red Ants' nest, announces his intention to undertake 'its geography and history, if not *ab urbe condita* then from our discovery of it'.

Ad astra per alia porci
To the stars on a pig's wings

The young John Steinbeck was told by his tutor that pigs would fly before he became a successful writer. He subsequently and gleefully made sure that the words *Ad astra per alia porci* appeared on the title page of each of his books.

cf. per ardua ad astra

Addenda
Things which are to be added

The endings '-anda' and '-enda' denote the gerundive of the verb, indicating that something has to be done (agenda, corrigenda, propaganda, pudenda, vivenda, etc.). 'Addenda' is plural: if a single item only has to be added, this is an 'addendum'.

Adeste fideles
Come, ye faithful

The first line of the Latin version of the hymn 'O come, all ye faithful', with music formerly thought to be composed by John Reading (*ob*. 1692), organist at Winchester College and author of *Dulce Domum*. It is now believed that the hymn was composed in 1743 by John Frances Wade.

Ad hoc
For this (special purpose)

An ad hoc committee, as opposed to a standing committee, is set up to consider a specific issue or problem. When the issue has been resolved or the problem solved, the ad hoc committee is disbanded.

> 'A paramedic is employed on an ad-hoc [sic] basis, whenever he is needed.'
>
> Report in *The Cornishman*

The phrase should be used with circumspection. A statement that 'the matter will be investigated by an ad hoc public inquiry' sounds sensible enough until one asks how an 'ad hoc' inquiry differs from an ordinary inquiry, since both must sooner or later present their report and then be disbanded.

Ad infinitum
To infinity

The discovery of the microscope gave mankind a new insight into the dimensions of comparative size, and provided a glimpse into hitherto unseen vistas of life (animalcules) on earth. As a result several microscopists claimed that:

> 'Great fleas have little fleas
> Upon their backs to bite 'em,
> And little fleas have lesser fleas,
> And so *ad infinitum*.'
>
> Augustus de Morgan, 'A Budget of Paradoxes'

Ad libitum (ad lib)
At pleasure

In a stage play, an ad lib is a line or comment which does not appear in the script, but which the actor speaks notwithstanding, at his own pleasure if not at that of the director.

If you are offered something *ad libitum*, you are free to accept or to reject the offer as you see fit. Written on a doctor's prescription, the abbreviation 'ad lib' means 'to be taken freely'.

Ad majorem Dei gloriam (AMDG)
To the greater glory of God

This is the motto of the Society of Jesus (alias 'The Jesuits'), and also of St Ignatius College in Middlesex. It is a favourite dedication for war memorials, rolls of honour and stained glass windows up and down the land, as well as being the standard dedication for the compositions of Johann Sebastian Bach.

Ad nauseam
Until it makes you sick

The nausea is usually brought on by repetition.

> 'He undermined his best images by repeating them ad nauseam.'
>
> Art criticism in *The Observer*

A book review in *The Guardian* complained that Marco Pierre White rarely mentioned flavour or taste in his discussion of cooking. 'What he does bang on about, *ad nauseam*, is the look of a plate.'

Football Club Mottoes

Arte et labore
By skill and hard graft
Blackburn Rovers

Pro rege et lege
For the king and the law
Leeds United

Supera moras
Overcome delays (Get your finger out)
Bolton Wanderers

Vincit omnia industria
Hard work conquers everything
Bury

Audere est facere
He who dares, wins
Tottenham Hotspur

Consilio et animis

By wisdom and courage

Sheffield Wednesday

Nil satis nisi optimum

Nothing but the best is good enough

Everton

Superbia in proelio

Pride in battle

Manchester City

Victoria concordia crescit

Victory grows from harmony

Arsenal

Aegrotat
He is ill

Anyone too ill (or too nervous or too drunk) to sit the final examination for a university degree, but whose work has shown sufficient merit up to that point, may on that evidence be granted the degree: his (or her) name will appear on the pass list, accompanied by the word aegrotat.

Aetatis suae
Of his (or her) age

Strictly speaking this should, and sometimes does, read *anno aetatis suae* ('in the year of his age'). It is frequently shortened to *aetat* or even to *aet*. The phrase appears in any of these forms on many old tombstones and memorials.

It may even be shortened to 'atat'. It is recorded that John Gibbs of Clyst St George, Devon, died in 1652 'Atat plus minus 82', the 'plus minus' (or 'more or less') reminding us how easy it was before birth certificates became obligatory to forget one's exact age, especially after eighty-odd years.

Affidavit
He has declared upon oath

Or 'he has sworn on oath'. A written affidavit, properly signed and witnessed, is equivalent to a sworn testimony and is as good as (and infinitely preferable to) a personal appearance in the witness box.

Afflavit Deus et dissipantur
God breathed and they are scattered

These words were inscribed on a medal struck by order of Queen Elizabeth I to commemorate the defeat of the Spanish Armada, giving due credit to God but not necessarily thereby devaluing the contributions of Sir Francis Drake et al. Drake himself acknowledged God's part in his many successes by having the motto *Auxilio Divino* ('By divine aid') on his crest.

A fortiori

With stronger reason

'These criticisms of the employees must apply a fortiori to the employers whose orders after all the employees were simply carrying out.'

Report in *The Observer*

'Malebranche… was murdered… Leibnitz, being every way superior to Malebranche, one might, a fortiori, have counted on *his* being murdered… '

Thomas de Quincey,
'On Murder considered as one of the Fine Arts'

'He means… that she fears and despises the whole subject – and, *a fortiori*, its adherents.'

Julian Barnes, *Arthur and George*

'A fortiori' as used here has a faint odour of the non sequitur about it – what 'stronger reason' is in evidence?

Mr Barnes is on slightly firmer ground in the following passage from *Something to Declare*, in which he ponders how to explain Sartre's instance of an idiot who becomes a genius: 'And how, *a fortiori*, to explain it when the documentary evidence is thin… ?'

Agenda

Things to be acted upon

'Agenda' is the plural of 'agendum'. Being already plural, it has no plural of its own, but English ingenuity has supplied the deficiency with 'agendas' (which is infinitely preferable to 'agendae'). It does not suffer alone in its plurality; its woes are shared by 'data' (*q.v.*), 'strata' and 'media' which are also plural forms but are often treated as though they were singular.

Agnus Dei, qui tollis peccata mundi, miserere nobis

Lamb of God, who takest away the sins of the world, have mercy on us

The origin of the passage is John 1:29.

The *Agnus Dei* is frequently said or sung as part of the Communion Service of the Church of England, although it does not in fact appear in the Communion section of the *Book of Common Prayer*.

Agnus Dei is also the name given to a cake of wax or dough stamped with the figure of a lamb carrying the banner of the Cross, and distributed by the Pope on the Sunday after Easter.

Ecce agnus Dei qui tollit peccata mundi ('Behold the Lamb of God who takes away the sins of the world') is the motto of the Worshipful Company of Tallow Chandlers.

Alias (dictus)

At another time (under a different name)

We seem to be in danger of losing the useful word 'alias' to the unattractive Americanism 'aka' ('also known as'). The only thing to be said for 'aka' is that it might be used for contemporaneous aliases, when someone uses different names according to circumstances. If Yusuf Islam was formerly known as Cat Stevens but no longer chooses to use this name, then he would then be 'alias Cat Stevens'; if he is Yusuf Ali in private but Cat Stevens when performing, then, fair enough, he is 'aka Cat Stevens'.

Fortunately 'aka' has as yet no plural, so we are forced instead to use 'alias' in such statements as 'Jones travelled under a variety of aliases' (and as in the second sentence above) even though 'alias' has no plural in Latin.

Alibi
Elsewhere

To have an alibi is to be able to prove you were elsewhere when the crime was committed and are therefore innocent. Robin Goodfellow could put a girdle round about the earth in forty minutes but even at that speed he couldn't be in two places at once.

An alibi is not, and never has been, the same as a mere excuse, although a section of the English-speaking media is doing its best to hide the proper meaning of this noble word.

> "'Vell,' said Mr Weller, "now I s'pose he'll want to call some witnesses to speak to his character, or p'raps to prove a alleybi… I've got some friends as'll do either for him, but my adwice wud be this here – never mind the character, and stick to the alleybi. Nothing like a alleybi, Sammy, nothing."'
>
> Charles Dickens, *The Pickwick Papers*

Aliquando bonus dormitat Homerus

Even good Homer nods at times

Homer nodded off permanently a few centuries ago but the phrase is still pertinent today: for 'Homer' simply substitute the name of any cricket umpire. It is often used to excuse anyone's lapse of memory or inattention to detail, but it is in fact a variant on a critical remark of Horace, who, in *Ars Poetica* 359, says: *Indignor quandoque bonus dormitat Homerus* ('I deem it unworthy of him if Homer, usually good, nods for a moment'). Horace will happily accept human frailty in any artist, but Homer? Of him he expects only the best.

Gideon Haigh in *Silent Revolutions* tells of how Errol Hunte, a West Indian test cricketer, was usually referred to in *Wisden's Cricketers' Almanack* as R. L. Hunte. Haigh comments on this error: '*Quandoque bonus dormitat Homerus* of course.'

Alma Mater

Nourishing mother, foster mother

Young people removed from the bosom of their families at a tender age to be boarded out at a public school have no choice but to accept this school as an Alma Mater. My own minor grammar school had a school song which referred to the school as *nostra mater altera* ('our second mother'). This did no great harm, since ours was a day school and each day after school we went rejoicing back to our first mothers.

Alter ego

Second self, other self

'[Leicester] appeared daily to advance in the Queen's favour. He was perpetually by her side in council – willingly listened to in the moments of courtly recreation... the alter ego, as it seemed of the stately Elizabeth.'

Sir Walter Scott, *Kenilworth*

An alter ego could also be one who has full powers to act for another. However, the phrase is frequently used nowadays to indicate that someone from time to time takes on a different persona (*q.v.*): 'Once behind the wheel of his car, he reveals his alter ego.'

Alumnus
A foster son, a former student

This is the next generation down in the family of the Alma Mater, both *alumnus* and *alma* being derived from the same root. It is normally, though not exclusively, used of an Old Boy (or Girl, alumna) of a school, or of a graduate of a university.

Ambo
Both (together)

Ambo is used to indicate in a duologue or duet that both persons are to talk or sing together.

Angina pectoris
A pain in the chest

Angina was the Latin for 'quinsy', which is suppurative tonsillitis. Through association with 'anguish' (French, *angoisse*), 'angina' has come to mean 'pain', a pain in the region of the heart.

Anno Domini (AD)

In the year of our Lord

Anno Christi (AC - in the year of Christ), Anno Graciae (AG - in the year of Grace) and Anno Salutis (AS - in the year of Salvation) can be found on old tombstones and memorials, although AD (Anno Domini) is by far the most common.

In the Western world (which was a Roman world) for some centuries after the birth of Christ, dates were still reckoned in the Roman style *('ab urbe conditae')*. It was Dionysius Exiguus in the early sixth century who fixed the date of the Nativity (at AD 1 or AUC 754), but his computation was probably up to half a dozen years out, and Christ may actually have been born a bit before His time in about 5 BC.

At some time in the past somebody decided for no clear reason to link *anno Domini* with the onset of old age, and it can often be heard when a middle-aged person can think of no better excuse for his personal shortcomings. It also appears in print:

'His latest work shows lamentable signs of *Anno* [sic] *Domini*'

Book review in *The Guardian*

'Nothing really wrong with him – only *anno domini* [sic], but that's the most fatal complaint of all...'

James Hilton, *Goodbye, Mr Chips*

Annus horribilis
A horrible year

This is the opposite of *annus mirabilis* (*q.v.*), and the phrase appears to have been coined *c.*1985. *Annus horribilis* or 'year of horrors' was quoted by H.M. Queen Elizabeth II, referring to 1992. An earlier year, 1349, the year the Black Death struck Europe, was the *annus terribilis*.

'Gardeners writing off 2006 as their "annus horribilis".'

Headline in *The Cornishman*

Annus mirabilis
The year of wonders

The original 'Year of Wonders' was 1666, remarkable for the Great Fire of London and for British military successes over the Dutch. An interesting extension of the phrase is *dies mirabilis* (wonderful day), used by Geoffrey Lean writing in *The Observer* when he comments on the length of time it took 'to learn… to walk again, first with physiotherapists… then – *dies mirabilis* – with a Zimmer frame'.

It was John Dryden who, in his poem entitled '*Annus Mirabilis*', celebrated the miracles of 1666, in which the Dutch were defeated and London escaped total destruction by fire. Philip Larkin also wrote a poem with this same title but with a slightly different subject: 'Sexual intercourse began/in nineteen sixty-three…'

Ante
Before

In a game of poker, each player lays down a stake or forced bet, the 'ante', before the cards are dealt. 'Upping the ante' is to raise the amount to be laid down before the action begins. Mark Twain, in *Roughing It*, writes: 'I reckon I can't call my hand. Ante and pass the buck.'

'Ante' is also used in various compound phrases, e.g. antenatal, ante-room, ante-bellum ('pre-war', especially the American Civil War). The paradoxical-sounding 'ante-post' betting refers to bets placed prior to the overnight declaration stage of a race, usually 10 a.m. on the day before it takes place.

Ante meridiem (a.m.)

Before midday

This, together with p.m. (*q.v.*), makes up the 24-hour day.

One can but wonder what possessed the Western civilisations to decide that the new day began in the middle of the previous night. The civilisations of the Near East took the reasonable view that the day began at sunrise, at around 6 a.m. Western time. Thus in Acts 2:15, Peter sets the time of the Pentecostal descent of the Holy Spirit on the disciples at 'the third hour' or 9 a.m.

Living for a few years in East Africa, I rapidly grew used to the local (Arabic and African) method of counting time from sunrise at 6 a.m. and from sunset at 6 p.m., so that 9 a.m. was then (in Swahili) *'saa tatu ya siku'* ('hour three of the day') and 11 p.m. was *'saa tano ya usiku'* ('hour five of the night').

Anti

Against

Used in combination ('an anti-war protest') or as a free-standing adjective ('he was always very anti when he was at college').

During the Great Schism of the West, 1309–76, a succession of popes was elected in opposition to the pope in Rome. These popes resided in Avignon, and are known generally as the 'anti-popes'.

Apologia
A vindication, defence

In 1864 Cardinal John Newman wrote an account of his life and opinions under the title *Apologia pro Vita Sua* ('A defence of the conduct of his life'). Over the years the term 'apology' has acquired connotations of guilt, of *mea culpa* (*q.v.*), but the original 'apologia' was in no sense apologetic.

Sara Wheeler, reviewing in *The Guardian* a book on Iran, suggested that the book 'is, above all else, an apologia for the unifying underlying meaning of Islamic art'.

A posteriori
From events coming after

A posteriori reasoning identifies causes by studying results.

> 'That it was Yorick's and no one's else: – It was proved to be so, *a posteriori [sic]*, the day after, when Yorick sent a servant to my Uncle Toby's house, to enquire after it.'

> Laurence Sterne, *Tristram Shandy*

cf. a priori

Apparatus
Things prepared

A word adopted *in toto* into English from Latin. Its original meaning was 'something prepared' but its meaning was then extended to signify the equipment used in preparation. The word is curious in that being a fourth declension noun, *apparatus* as written may be either singular or plural. It is equally correct to say, 'The apparatus is broken', and 'The apparatus are broken'.

When I was in training for my spell of National Service, we were instructed how to fall flat on our faces preparatory to firing our rifles, 'being careful to avoid the wedding apparatus as you go down'.

A priori
From preceding events

A priori reasoning involves arguing from basic premises or from first principles, and seeing to what conclusion the arguments lead.

In the essay 'Is Theology Poetry?', C. S. Lewis considers modern naturalism: 'Does not the whole vast structure... depend... simply on an *a priori* metaphysical prejudice?'

cf. a posteriori

Aqua fortis
Strong water

This is not water at all but nitric acid, used by aquafortists engaged in engraving designs on copper.

Aqua regia
Royal water

Like *aqua fortis*, this is not water at all, but a mixture of one part of nitric with two to four parts of hydrochloric acid, which has the power to dissolve gold, the king of metals.

Aqua vitae
The water of life

Unlike *aqua fortis* and *aqua regia*, this is best taken by mouth, being some form of alcohol, usually brandy *(eau-de-vie)*. The Gaelic form of the phrase, *uisge-beatha*, gives us the word 'whisky', while the Scandinavians are said to drink a caraway-flavoured spirit called *akvavit*.

And yet it is said to be all a mistake, being the mis-rendering back into medieval Latin of the Spanish *acqua di vite* ('juice of the vine'). The correct translation would be 'aqua vitis', but who cares? 'Aqua vitae' is a very happy error.

Argumentum
ad hominem

An argument to the man

Not involving so much an appeal to a man's better nature, but appealing to his inner nature, calling up his own deeply-held views and principles in support of the argument:

> '… that soft and irresistible piano of voice, which the nature of the *argumentum ad hominem* absolutely requires …'
>
> Laurence Sterne, *Tristram Shandy*

The phrase *ad hominem* can also be applied to an attack made on a person's character so as to avoid having to counter his arguments.

Ars est celare artem

True art lies in concealing art

A Latin proverb. Ovid may have had it in mind when he said (in *Artis Amatoriae* 2:213) *Si latet ars, prodest* ('If the art is concealed, it succeeds'), the art here being the sly and subtle art of seduction.

Ars est celare artem was the motto chosen by the Central Signals Establishment of the RAF, but presumably not for its seductive implications.

Ars gratia artis
Art for art's sake

Théophile Gautier (1811–72) coined the slogan *L'art pour l'art*, which was taken up by Walter Pater and others in the Aesthetic movement in Britain, and rendered as 'Art for art's sake'. The Latin version has become familiar to millions as the legend around the roaring lion (Leo) of the Metro-Goldwyn-Mayer films.

Ars longa, vita brevis
Art is long, life is short, or So long a time to learn the art, so short a time to live

Seneca quoted Hippocrates as saying this, in *De Brevitate Vitae (Of the Brevity of Life)*. The art was the art of healing, as one might suppose of Hippocrates. The phrase does *not* mean, as suggested in the schoolboy howler, 'a short skirt on a fat bottom', although *Punch* magazine once added its own comment to an obituary notice: 'John Longbottom, aged 3 months, dies: *Ars longa vita brevis.*'

In *Doctor in the House*, Richard Gordon states that over the entrance to St Swithin's Hospital was engraved 'Hippocrates' discouraging aphorism'.

Aurora australis
Dawn in the south – the Southern Lights

Aurora is the pink glow in the eastern sky heralding the dawn. *Auster* was the south wind; Australia is the southern continent, originally designated as *Terra Australis Incognita*.

Aurora borealis
Dawn in the north – the Northern Lights

Boreas was the north wind.

Ave atque vale

Hail and farewell

Catullus, visiting his brother's tomb near Troy for the first time while on his way to Bithynia, and not expecting to pass that way again, says in *Carmina* 101:10: *Atque in perpetuum, frater, ave atque vale* ('And so for ever, brother, hail and farewell'). Alfred Lord Tennyson wrote a poem entitled 'Frater Ave atque Vale', and A. C. Swinburne wrote a poem with 'Ave atque Vale' as its title, in memory of Baudelaire.

Up to the end of the 1920s the termly magazine of my grammar school used 'Ave atque Vale' for the list of names of those pupils who had either just entered the school or just left it.

Colin Dexter heads the final chapter of *The Jewel that was Ours* with the last two lines of the poem: *Accipe fraterno multum manantia fletu/Atque in perpetuum, frater, ave atque vale* ('Accept [these gifts] much drenched with a brotherly tear, And so, [etc.]… ').

Ave Maria

Hail Mary

In Luke 1:28 the Archangel Gabriel addresses Mary with these words: 'Hail, thou that art highly favoured, the Lord is with thee, blessed art thou among women.' The Vulgate has *Ave gratia plena, Dominus tecum* ('Hail, full of grace, the Lord is with thee'). In neither of these versions does the angel mention Mary by name, and the habit arose later of making it clear exactly who the highly-favoured lady was. The version to be found for example in the Visconti *Book of Hours* has the angel say explicitly: *Ave Maria gratia plena* ('Hail Mary, full of grace').

The passage was a prayer to be repeated a set number of times as penance after Confession. In the rosary, the small beads were known as Ave Maria beads, distinct from the larger paternoster (*q.v.*) beads. The Ave Maria bell was sounded at six o'clock and twelve o'clock to invite the faithful to repeat the prayer.

City of London Livery Company mottoes:

Amore sitis uniti
Be united in love
Tinplate Workers alias Wire Workers Company

Corde recto elati omnes
All are uplifted by a righteous heart
Makers of Playing Cards Company

Decus et tutamen
A handsome protection in war
Feltmakers' Company

Hinc spes effulget
Hope shines out of here
Innholders' Company

Lucem tuam da nobis Deus
O God give us your light
Glaziers' Company

Omnia subjectisti sub pedibus oves et boves

You have put everything under his feet, including sheep and cattle

Butchers' Company

Producat terra

The earth produces

Tobacco Pipe Makers and Tobacco Blenders' Company

Verbum Domini manet in aeternum

The word of the Lord endures for ever

Stationers and Newspaper Makers' Company

Bona fide
In good faith, legitimate

A 'bona fide' (with or without a hyphen) offer is one made in good faith, without intention to deceive.

At one time, pubs were allowed to serve drinks out of hours only to persons on a journey.

> 'I reminded them that all public-houses were closed till six o'clock. Stillwood said: "That's all right – *bona-fide* travellers."'
> G. and W. Grossmith, *The Diary of a Nobody*

> '... Twisdon would prove his *bona fides* by passing the word "Black Stone" and whistling "Annie Laurie".'
> John Buchan, *The Thirty-Nine Steps*

To question someone's *bona fides* is to be suspicious of his intentions, of his good faith. In one of A. P. Herbert's *Misleading Cases*, the 'Reasonable Man' is defined as one who 'investigates exhaustively the *bona fides* of every mendicant before distributing alms'.

Camera obscura
A darkened room

Not the 'dark room' in which film is developed, but a darkish room, sometimes a mere box, in which an image from the outside world is projected via a series of lenses on to a screen.

Carpe diem
Reap the harvest of the day

The complete thought, as written by Horace in *Odes*, is *Carpe diem quam minimum credula postero* ('Reap the harvest of the day, trust as little as possible in the morrow').

Many poets have written poems in the spirit of 'Gather ye rosebuds while ye may' and 'Youth's a stuff will not endure'. Byron uses the phrase in the last stanza of 'Don Juan':

'But *carpe diem*, Juan, *carpe, carpe*!
Tomorrow sees another race as gay
And transient, and devour'd by the same harpy...'

Casus belli

A reason for war, for dispute

The invasion of Belgium in 1914, that of Poland in 1939, and the threat of weapons of mass destruction in Iraq at a later date, are each an example of a *casus belli*. The term can also be used in a less destructive sense. Adrian Hamilton, writing in *The Observer*, says: 'Yesterday the *casus belli* was the Social Charter, today it is the budget.'

Casus, like 'apparatus', is a fourth declension noun and the plural of *casus belli* is also *casus belli*.

'[An inquiry dealt with] hedge-scouring and whin-drawing (and a hundred other obscure *casus belli* between landlord and tenant).'

John Fowles, *A Maggot*

Caveat

Let him beware

If I am empowered to issue a caveat on a particular matter, then no one may act on that matter without letting me know first. On the other hand, the word now seems to be used as a synonym for 'warning'. Writing in *The Observer*, Janet Watts predicted that Somerville College would eventually become mixed: 'Amid gallantries to the young women and caveats to the college… '

Caveat emptor
Let the buyer beware

A maxim in Latin law, and of perennial and universal relevance.

> 'eBay itself is plastered with "caveat emptor" warnings.'
>
> Letter in The Guardian

The reader may also be vulnerable. Also in *The Guardian*, Sara Wheeler, reviewing a book on Iran, mentions a long essay on the origins and history of Islamic art, before which the author 'inserts a caveat lector advising uninterested readers to skip to the next chapter'.

Cave canem
Beware of the dog

This famous warning, quoted by Petronius but dating back to the Greeks, was discovered written in mosaic on the portal of a house excavated in the ruins of Pompeii.

Ceteris paribus
Other things being equal

'*Ceteris paribus*, I think we'd better be going.'
> Rudyard Kipling, 'The Puzzler'

'A very rich man, from low beginnings, may buy his election in a borough; but *caeteris paribus* a man of family will be preferred.'
> Dr Samuel Johnson

Circa (c. or ca.)
About

Usually with reference to a point in time, time being a fluid quantity difficult to pin down.

'The Celtic drive southwards down the Italian Peninsula was paralleled by another one *ca*.350 BC into the Balkans and Greece.'
> D. B. Gregor, *Celtic*

Of the two abbreviations, *c.* is now preferred.

Citius, Altius, Fortius

Faster, higher, stronger

Latin was chosen for the motto of the Olympic Games,
presumably because it was a neutral language.

Coitus interruptus

Interrupted intercourse

Specifically a method of birth control by withdrawing
before ejaculation. The withdrawal need not be
voluntary.

'On the night of the murder she had a client in bed
with her, and if ever there was a *locus classicus* for
what they call *coitus interruptus* this was it, because
someone interrupted the proceedings.'

Colin Dexter, *The Remorseful Day*

Compos mentis
Of sound mind

Literally, 'in complete possession of (one's) reason', or in full possession of one's mental faculties. The phrase was used by Cicero and is now a legal term.

cf. non compos mentis

Confederatio Helvetica (CH)

The Helvetican Confederation (Switzerland)

'CH' is the International Vehicle Registration allocated to Switzerland and can be seen on the rear of Swiss cars and on their number plates. The abbreviation for Swiss Francs is 'chf' and the Internet domain for Switzerland is 'ch'.

Helvetia is the Latin name for Switzerland, home of the *Helvitii*, a powerful Celtic people. Since in all the four languages used in the country the name for Switzerland begins with 'S', it is not prima facie clear why 'S' could not be used instead of 'CH', until one realises that Sweden got there first, just beating Switzerland to it in alphabetical order. 'SW' would not have done instead (Schweiz, Suisse, Svizzera, etc.) so 'CH' is a good compromise, and Latin is a nice, neutral language.

Confer (cf.)
Compare

Confer is the imperative of *conferre*. In the past the English word 'confer' meant 'compare', in the sense of bringing two things together.

Consensus
Agreement, unanimity

This has nothing to do with 'census' and everything to do with 'consent', so there can really be no excuse for misspelling it.

Consummatum est
It is finished

The last words of Christ on the Cross (John 19:30). Marlowe puts the same words into the mouth of Dr Faustus as he signs the bill of sale of his soul to Lucifer.

Contra (con)
Against

'Contra-' is generally used in compound words such as 'contradict', 'contraflow' and 'contraindication'.

Cornucopia

*The horn of plenty, a source
of unlimited wealth*

Originally *cornu copiae,* referring to the horn of the goat by which Zeus was suckled. The grateful Zeus rather unkindly wrenched a horn from the goat and gave it to the goat's owner, promising that the horn would thenceforth be empowered 'to scatter plenty o'er a smiling land'.

Corpus

Body

Literally a body in the phrase *Habeas corpus (q.v.),* but also used metaphorically, as when 'corpus' refers to a body of work on a particular subject by different authors. Roy Jenkins, reviewing in *The Observer* a biography of Sir John Simon, mentions 'the large corpus of anti-Simon invective'.

Corpus delicti
The body of the crime

The *corpus delicti* does not have to be a corpse. It could be a snatched handbag found on the person of the snatcher, or a burnt-out building after an arson attack. Whatever it is, living or dead, it must present clear evidence that a crime has been committed.

Corrigenda
Things to be corrected

Usually twinned with *addenda* (*q.v.*). The singular is 'corrigendum'. In English publications 'addenda and corrigenda' are the remedy for 'errors and omissions' (although in the reverse order).

Credo
I believe

Credo gives us our English word 'creed', and is the first word of the Creed of the Latin Mass: *Credo in unum Deum…* ('I believe in one God… ')

The word is also used for the totality of a person's beliefs, secular as well as religious.

Cui bono (fuerit)?
To whom is the profit? or Who stands to gain?

Cicero quotes Lucius Cassius Longinus, a judge, who asked this question in the search for a motive behind whatever illegal action he was looking into. The phrase does *not* mean 'What good does it do?'

Cum
With

Used as a linking word, as in 'The Parish of Winkworth-cum-Hobberton Magna'. In *The Observer* Andrew Motion, reviewing a book by Konrad Lorenz, referred to it as 'an autobiography-cum-diary-cum-analysis'.

Cum grano (salis)
With a pinch (of salt)

Pliny in his *Naturalis Historia* told of how a grain of salt was a key ingredient in an antidote to a poison; now it is in itself an antidote to undue credulity.

A character in Ernest Bramah's 'The Secret of Headland Height' comments on the tradition of an early British chief or king being buried in a gold coffin: 'Personally, I take it *cum grano*.'

Cum privilegio
With licence

A phrase to be found on the title page of certain books, especially bibles and prayer books, published by leave of the appropriate authorities.

Curriculum Vitae (CV)
Course of life, life history

A *curriculum* was originally a chariot, and by extension came to mean the course along which chariot races were run. A school curriculum outlines the course of study that its students follow, while a curriculum vitae maps the course of one's life to date. Dame Muriel Spark gave the title *Curriculum Vitae* to her autobiography.

Da mihi castitatem et continentiam, sed noli modo

Grant me chastity and continence –
but not just yet

These are not the words of our own St Augustine of Canterbury 'with his feet of snow', but of a more flamboyant St Augustine of Hippo in what is now Algeria, who lived two centuries earlier (AD 354–430). The prayer, quoted in his *Confessions*, was uttered while he was engaged to be married but was still enjoying the comforts afforded first by a concubine and then by a new love. Shortly after this, however, he was converted to Christianity and became a (celibate) priest.

Data

Given facts

Facts which are accepted, which are acknowledged to be true. The word 'data' is plural:

C. S. Lewis, in 'Is Theology Poetry?', suggests that the disputants are 'not really starting with the *datum* "Both are poetical" and thence arguing "Therefore both are false".'

A 'datum-line' is a 'given' horizontal line from which heights and depths are measured. Until 1921 the datum line for Great Britain was the mean sea level at Liverpool. Since 1921 it has been the mean sea level at Newlyn, Cornwall.

De facto
In fact

It is not uncommon in troubled times for a country to have two governments, the *de jure* (in law, legal) government, properly elected by law but forced to function in exile, and the de facto government, not elected but firmly *in situ* in the country and running its day-to-day affairs and collecting taxes.

In Australia a de facto wife is equivalent to what we know in Britain as a common law wife.

De gustibus non est disputandum
There is no arguing about taste

An old Latin proverb.

Dei gratia (DG)
By the grace of God

It has to be conceded that British monarchs were on the whole creditably modest about their claims to greatness and majesty, and the letters 'DG' impressed on the coinage advertised their acute and grateful awareness that, but for the grace of God, they would be no more than common citizens or worse.

Delirium tremens (dt's)
The trembling fever

The dt's are a symptom of one of the final stages in the drunkard's steady progress towards an early grave.

De minimis non curat lex
The law does not concern itself with trivialities
(literally 'with the smallest things')

The quotation comes from Francis Bacon, *Letter* 282.

'Whenever a fellow called Rex
Flashed his very small organ of sex,
He always got off,
For the judges would scoff,
"De minimis non curat lex".'

anon.

De mortuis nil nisi bonum (dicendum est)

Let nothing but good be said of the dead

Diogenes Laertius (AD *c*.200–250) mentions this phrase in *The Lives and Opinions of Eminent Philosophers*, attributing it to Chilon, one of the 'Seven Sages' of Greece.

> '… there was praise… for the victim, as if *De mortuis* was engraved on every county heart.'
>
> John Fowles, 'The Enigma'

Dr Johnson was all in favour of being generous to the dead in writing their epitaphs: 'In lapidary inscriptions a man is not upon oath.'

The phrase does *not* mean, as suggested in the schoolboy howler, 'When you're dead, there ain't nothing left but bones.'

Denarius (d.)

Penny

In 1086 the only coin in circulation in Britain was the silver penny. 'Penny', like *pfennig*, is a Germanic word: the Latin name *denarius*, shortened to 'd.' as in '3d.' for threepence, stuck until 1971. The *denarius* also mutated into *dinar*, in use today in Algeria, Bahrain, Iraq, Jordan, Kuwait, Libya, Tunisia and Yugoslavia. *Dineros* is still the Spanish for 'money'. The equivalent Portuguese word is *dinheiro*.

The French also adopted the *denarius* under the eventual name *denier* for a small coin of little value, twelve of which were worth one sou, just as twelve British pennies were worth one shilling. Shakespeare knew of the coin, making Richard II say 'My dukedom to a beggarly denier' (*Richard II* 1:3).

The *denier*, like the penny, was also used as a measure of weight, and the term is still used to measure the weight of fine thread, such as silk and nylon; 15-denier nylon stockings are made from thread which weighs 15 grams per 9000 metres.

Deo gratias
Thanks be to God

The closing words of the Mass, used also at various points during the service, such as after the Epistle and after the last Gospel.

> 'Brother Nick has at last decided to mend the lorry. *Deo gratias.*'
>
> Iris Murdoch, *The Bell*

Deo optimo maximo (DOM)
To God, most good, most great.

At last, the real meaning of the letters DOM which appear on bottles of Benedictine. *Deo optimo maximo* is the motto of the Benedictine Order.

Deo volente (DV)
God willing

> '"And," said Caroline, "you will promise to come to my table, and to sit near me, Mr Hall?" "I shall not fail, Deo volente," said he.'
>
> Charlotte Brontë, *Shirley*

De profundis
Out of the depths

The first two words in Latin of Psalm 130: *De profundis clamavi ad te, Domine: Domine, exaudi vocem meam* ('Out of the depths have I cried unto thee, O Lord: Lord, hear my voice').

In 1905 Oscar Wilde wrote an *Apologia pro sua vita* called *De Profundis*. Both Robert Browning and Elizabeth Barrett Browning wrote poems with this same title, as did C. S. Lewis and Garcia Lorca.

> '*De profundis clamavi*, from the depths of this repulsive hotel bedroom… I call to you.'
>
> Aldous Huxley, *Point Counter Point*

De Profundis is the motto of the Urban District Council of Bedlington in Northumberland, in a former coal-mining area.

Desiderata
Things to be desired

The singular is *desideratum*. Woody Allen in his story 'Retribution' describes Connie Chasen who, through 'the lewd, humid eroticism her every curve suggested... was the unrivalled *desideratum* of each young man'.

Deus ex machina
A god from the machine

In Greek drama this was a god lowered by a pulley from above the stage to take an unexpected hand in the action, and was a device much favoured, especially by Euripides. In a less literal form it is still a very handy device for resolving an impasse in a drama, where a quite independent agent acts arbitrarily in an unpredictable and often improbable way.

In John Fowles' 'The Enigma', Isobel Dodgson talks of the need for a story to have a credible ending and proposes 'to dismiss the *deus ex machina* possibility. It's not good art. An awful cheat, really.'

Section 10 of Fougasse and McCullough's book *You Have Been Warned* has the title *Dea in Machina* ('A goddess in the machine'). It records the emotions of a driver who offers a lift in his car to a strikingly beautiful girl and against all hope has the offer accepted.

Dies irae, dies illa …
That day is a day of wrath…

In his biblical prophecy (Zephaniah 1:15), Zephaniah warned that the great day of the Lord was near, a day of wrath, of 'trouble and distress', of 'wasteness and desolation', and sundry other forms of unpleasantness.

In the thirteenth century Thomas of Celano put this idea into verse of some seventeen or more stanzas. For many years this poem was part of the Requiem Mass for the Dead, but in 1970 it was removed from the Mass, for fear that its message of doom and despair might frighten the faithful.

Disjecta membra
Dismembered limbs

Ovid in his *Metamorphoses* wrote of *disjecta membra* – 'scattered limbs'.

Byron wrote to his publisher, John Murray, about *Don Juan*: 'Cut me up root and branch – quarter me in the *Quarterly* – send round my *disjecti membra poetae*… but don't ask me to alter it.'

'I can hardly see what use the *disjecta membra* of my late acquaintance [*viz* the bones of a goose] are going to be to me.'

Sir Arthur Conan Doyle,
The Adventures of Sherlock Holmes

Domine, dirige nos
Lord, lead us

The word *dirige* is the first word of an antiphon sung in the Office for the Dead, taken from Psalm 5:8: 'Lead me, Lord, in thy righteousness.' It gave the English language the word 'dirge' for a sad musical tribute to the dead.

Domine dirige nos is the motto of the City of London.

Dominus illuminatio mea
The Lord is my light

These words appear in Psalm 27. They are also the motto of the University of Oxford and appear on the colophon of that city's University Press.

In *The Oxford Book of English Verse*, the title *Dominus illuminatio mea* is given to R. D. Blackmore's poem, 'In the hour of death, after this life's whim'.

Dominus vobiscum
The Lord be with you

This, from the Ordinary of the Mass of the Roman Catholic Church, has the response: *Et cum spiritu tuo* – 'And with thy spirit'. The English version of the two phrases appears in the Book of Common Prayer *passim*.

Dominus Vobiscum is also a beer brewed in Quebec.

cf. pax vobiscum

Dramatis personae
The characters of a play

The traditional heading of a cast list. 'Persona' was the name given to the mask worn by a Roman actor.

Dulce et decorum est
pro patria mori

It is sweet and proper to die for one's country

Tempora mutantur, and Wilfred Owen writing nearly two thousand years after Horace's *Odes* 3:2:13, took an understandably different view of death in battle. Owen describes in his poem 'Dulce et Decorum' the effects of mustard gas in the trenches in France in the Great War.

'If you could hear, at every jolt, the blood
Come gargling from the froth-corrupted lungs…
My friend, you would not tell with such high zest
To children ardent for some desperate glory
The old Lie: Dulce et decorum est
Pro patria mori.'

Dum spiro spero

While I have breath I have hope

For centuries this defiant motto has dropped from the lips of members of the MacLennan clan, and has also been adopted in the course of time by several dozen prominent families, including those of Bannatyne of Newhall, Coryton of Pentillic Castle and Jackson of Putney Hill. It is also the motto of St Andrews in Scotland. In 1776 the line *Dum spiro, spero* was incorporated into the Great Seal of the state of South Carolina, and it is also the proud boast of the Kingdom of Sarawak.

School Mottoes

Coelesti luce crescat
It grows with celestial light
Cheltenham Ladies' College

Discendo duces
By learning you will lead
Newcastle-upon-Tyne Grammar School

Finis coronat opus
The end crowns the work
Croham Hurst School, Croydon

Veritas sine timore
Truth without fear
Caterham School

Ecce homo
Behold the man

Under this title Guido Reni, among other artists, painted Christ crowned with thorns.

> 'Then came Jesus forth, wearing the crown of thorns, and the purple robe. And Pilate saith unto them, Behold the man!'
>
> John 19:5

Elizabeth Regina (ER)
Queen Elizabeth

Queen Elizabeth II's monogram appears on post boxes and elsewhere as EIIR.

Emeritus
Having earned one's retirement

Especially, a retired professor, who, through the title of 'Emeritus Professor', is allowed to retain a little of the glory attaching to his previous post.

It is said that Rupert Murdoch dubbed a sacked editor as 'emeritus' – '"E" means you're out, "meritus" means you deserve it.'

E pluribus unum

From many [comes] the one

The motto of the United States of America from 1782 until 1956 (replaced then by 'In God We Trust'), this phrase was adapted from one used by Virgil in his *Moretum*.

Variants on this motto are popular. *E duobus unum* ('One from two') is the motto of the Welding Institute, and also of the Corinthian Casuals Football Club, formed in 1939 by the amalgamation of the Corinthians and the Casuals football clubs.

Ergo
Therefore

cf. post hoc ergo propter hoc

Errata
Errors

The singular is 'erratum'.

Patrick Ness, writing in *The Guardian* of a copy he had bought of a first edition of Alasdair Gray's *Unlikely Stories, Mostly*, rejoices that 'it still contains Gray's famous fake *erratum* slip ("This slip has been inserted by mistake")'.

Et alii (et al.)
And others

Usually written (and spoken) as 'et al.', it could stand not only for *et alii* (masculine) but also for *et aliae* (feminine). The neuter would be *et alia* but for this *et cetera* (*q.v.*) is preferred.

Et cetera (etc.)
And the others, and the rest

Et in Arcadia ego
I too [have lived] in Arcadia

This inscription appears on the tomb in Poussin's painting of 'The Arcadian Shepherds', as well as in paintings by Guercino and Bartolomeo Schidoni. An alternative reading is 'Even in Arcady am I' – that is, Death.

Evelyn Waugh gives the heading *Et in Arcadia ego* to the first part of his *Brideshead Revisited*. Arcadia was a district of the Peloponnesus inhabited largely by shepherds and other rustics, and according to Virgil was an area noted for its pastoral simplicity and happiness.

Robert Louis Stevenson wrote a poem with the title '*Et tu in Arcadia vixisti*' ('You too have lived in Arcadia').

Et sequens (et seq.)
And following

A term (sometimes just *seq*) used especially with a page reference, noting that the pages following are also relevant: 'Bennett, *op. cit.*, p. 209 *et seq.*'

Ex astris scientia
Knowledge from the stars

This was the motto of Starfleet Academy in the television series *Star Trek*.

Ex cathedra

From a chair, with authority

An *ex cathedra* announcement or judgement is one against which there can really be precious little hope of argument or appeal, such is the overwhelming authority of the person making the statement. In the Roman Catholic Church the author of *ex cathedra* announcements is the Pope, wearing his traditional cloak of infallibility.

Julian Barnes, in *Something to Declare*, speaks disparagingly of a certain 'moral thumpiness' intensified 'by the use of organ and backing choir, not to mention the spoken *ex cathedra* pronouncement'.

Exeat

Let him go out

Permission granted to a priest by his bishop to leave his diocese, or to an undergraduate to leave university during term.

Exempli gratia (e.g.)
For example

Literally 'by way of example'. *Gratia* was a Latin word of several uses, generally connected with doing someone a favour: *vide*, e.g. 'ex gratia', 'gratis'. The phrase *exempli gratia* was used by Cicero in the sense we recognise today.

Exeunt (omnes)
They (all) go out

A common stage direction. *Exeunt* is the plural of *exit*.

Ex gratia
By kindness

The victim of a mishap may have no legal claim for damages against the author of the mishap, who may nonetheless, purely out of the goodness of his heart, or for other undisclosed motives, make an ex gratia payment in compensation to the victim, without thereby admitting any liability.

Exit

He goes out

Sometimes hastily, as in Shakespeare's *The Winter's Tale* 3:3, where a well-known stage direction reads: '*Exit* pursued by a bear.'

Ex libris

From the books (or library) of

The usual inscription on a book plate pasted on the inside cover and displaying one's name as a safeguard against losing one's books by lending them to forgetful friends.

It was once the practice for children to write after their name inside the front cover of each of their school books a Latin poem: *Hic liber est meus, Testis est Deus. Si quis furetur, Per collem pendetur* ('This book is mine, A witness is God. If anyone steals this, By the neck he shall be hung'). The whole was usually finished off tastefully with a sketch of a body on a gallows.

Ex nihilo nihil fit
Nothing comes of nothing

This is a distillation of a statement of Lucretius in *De Rerum Natura* 1:155 – *Nil posse creari de nilo* ('Nothing can be created out of nothing').

In *A Short History of Myth*, Karen Armstrong discusses a poem which deals with how certain gods themselves first came into being: 'There is no creation *ex nihilo* but an evolutionary process… '

Ex officio
By virtue of office

'… the camp cook – a most important member of the outfit – had straddled his bronco and departed, being unable to withstand the fire of fun and practical jokes of which he was, ex-officio, the legitimate target.'

O. Henry, 'The Marquis and Miss Sally'

Ex parte
From one side

An *ex parte* statement presents only one side of an argument. It is the opposite of impartial. To call an account of an event 'partial' is ambiguous; but the partiality of an *ex parte* account can be in no doubt.

Ex post facto
In retrospect, retrospectively

An *ex post facto* law allows the conviction and punishment retrospectively of someone who commits an act before it becomes an offence in law.

Extempore
Made up at the time, without preparation

That is, made up on the spur of the moment, spoken 'off the cuff' (in the days when gentlemen orators wore starched white shirt-cuffs on which they could jot down notes a minute or so before they rose to their feet to speak). The term was used by Cicero.

Facsimile
Make the same

At one time a hyphenated word, 'fac-simile', this term denotes an exact copy of handwriting, or of a coin or similar object. The 'facsimile transmission' of documents electronically is now popularly known as 'fax'.

Factotum
Do everything

A Jack-of-all-trades, a general handyman. Figaro was the factotum of all the town. (In Latin the two words are separate: *fac totum*.)

Faex populi
The dregs of the people

One level lower than the plebs. The plural of *faex* is *faeces*.

Fauna
Wildlife

Usually the wildlife of a region, but excluding the plant life (*cf. flora*). The word *fauna* is Latin for a tutelary deity or guardian god of shepherds, which we have taken into English as 'faun' and which the French have as *faune*.

In *Sweet Thursday*, John Steinbeck introduces Fauna, the madame of the Bear Flag establishment. Previously she had run a mission for down-and-outs, and had been called Flora, but she adopted the name Fauna after 'a gentleman bum' had said, 'Flora, you seem more like a fauna-type to me.'

Fecit
He made

An author might sign off at the end of his work: *Adolphus Smith fecit*. The work in question could be written or it could be composed in some other medium: e.g. the Blarney Stone commemorates the builder of Blarney Castle, and is inscribed: 'Cormac Mac Carthy *fortis me fieri fecit* a.d [sic] 1446' ('Cormac Mac Carthy had me built strong').

Felix qui potuit rerum cognoscere causas

Happy is he who has been able to find out the causes of things

The phrase comes from Virgil's *Georgics* 2:490.

The London School of Economics has the motto *Rerum cognoscere causas*. The college was always among the avant-garde of its day, especially in ladies' fashion, and before the Second World War it was known to its sister colleges of London University as: '*Rerum cognoscere causas*, The place where women wear trousers.'

Felix qui potuit is the motto of Sir William Carew of Devon, and *Rerum cognoscere causas* is also the motto of Sheffield University and of the Institute of Brewing, with hints of mystery ingredients in beer.

Ferae naturae

Of a wild nature

Sometimes by extension used to mean 'wild animals'.

Just for the record and solely by way of illustration, John Dryden in 'The Mock Astrologer' avers that 'women are not comprised in our Laws of Friendship: they are *ferae naturae*'.

Festina lente
Hasten slowly

Presumably because 'More haste, less speed'. The phrase comes from Suetonius. It advises caution rather than procrastination. We are told that in its Greek form this was a favourite saying of Augustus Caesar. We are also told it was a favourite of Erasmus.

The Festina Lente Foundation is based at Bray in Hampshire and offers training in equestrianism and horticulture, both of these being skills which presumably cannot be learned in a hurry.

Fiat
Let it be

In *Villette*, Charlotte Brontë speaks of blanks in her heroine's life, 'the result of circumstances, the fiat of fate, a part of my life's lot'.

Fiat lux
Let there be light

'And God said, Let there be light: and there was light.'
Genesis 1:3

Fiat lux is the motto of the Moorfields Eye Hospital in London. It is also a popular title with film-makers and with firms producing lighting equipment.

Fidei defensor
(fid. def., FD)
Defender of the faith

Henry VIII was very flattered to be designated Defender of the Faith by Pope Leo X in 1521, in recognition of his diatribe against Martin Luther, although later, following a small disagreement in 1533 over the marital status of Queen Catherine of Aragon, Pope Paul III revoked the title. The King continued to use it, however, and set up his own version of the faith, becoming head of the Church of England. Parliament later conferred the title 'Defender of the Faith' on Henry's son, Edward VI, and to this day his successors to the crown have so described themselves on the coinage of the realm and elsewhere.

Finis
The end

Books are still published whose last word on the last page is *Finis*.

Flora

The goddess of flowers

Flora started life as a nymph, Chloris, who was ravished by Zephyr, the spring breeze and, being thus disqualified from being a nymph, was transmuted into the goddess. The whole episode is succinctly presented by Botticelli on the right hand side of his painting *La Primavera* ('Spring').

> 'O, for a draught of vintage! that hath been
> Cool'd a long time in the deep-delved earth,
> Tasting of Flora and the country green… '
>
> John Keats, 'Ode to a Nightingale'

'Flora' is used generally to denote the plant life of a region.

cf. fauna

Floreat

May it flourish

This is the first word of the motto of Eton College: *Floreat Etona* ('May Eton flourish'). Other (sometimes less illustrious) establishments use the same formula for their mottoes, such as *Floreat Actona* (London Borough of Acton), *Floreat Kew*, *Floreat Swansea* and *Floreat Salopia* (Shropshire).

Floruit (fl.)
Flourished

When the date of birth of a painter or author or other creative artist is unknown, this label is used to indicate the period in which he was known to be pursuing his art. 'Giovanni di Paolo (*fl.* 1420–85)' is a case in point.

Focus
Hearth

Until we all invested in central heating and television, the fire burning on the hearth was the centre of any household. Whereas in English we talk now only of the 'focus of attention' or of 'focusing' a lens, *focus* gives the French their word not only for the hearth, *foyer*, but also for the fire within it, *feu*. The focus of a lens in French is also *foyer*. The Italians use *fuoco* to mean both 'fire' and 'focus'.

Fons et origo
The source and origin

Literally, *fons* is a fountain or spring. *Fons et Origo* is the motto of the La Fontaine family.

'… you have the privilege of knowing one of the most complete young blackguards about town, and the *fons et origo* of the whole trouble.'

E. W. Hornung, *Raffles*

Gaudeamus igitur, juvenes dum sumus

Let us rejoice therefore, while we are still young

The opening words of a song which I found first in *The Scottish Students' Songbook*. It has been sung by students throughout Europe over the centuries and is also known under the title *De Brevitate Vitae* ('On the Shortness of Life'). It is set to music composed AD *c*.1267 by Strada, Bishop of Bologna. Brahms quotes the tune in his 'Academic Festival Overture'.

It is sadly unlikely that this phrase gave rise to the term 'Gaudy', an academic and frequently rowdy entertainment at certain universities, but the verb *gaudire* ('to rejoice') is the common source of the two 'g' words.

Genius loci

The spirit or god of a place

In a bygone era, and in a place where every natural feature of the land had its own tutelary deity, this would have been a local god. Virgil in the *Aeneid* 7:136, says *Geniumque loci invocat* ('And he prays to the god of the place').

'We had a comfortable supper, and got into high spirits. I felt all my toryism glow in this old capital of Staffordshire. I could have offered incense *genio loci*.'

James Boswell, *The Life of Samuel Johnson, LL.D*

Genus

A group of closely related species

A genus is general but a species (*q.v.*) is special, and a species is a sub-division of a genus. For example, modern man is *Homo sapiens* (*q.v. infra*), *Homo* being the genus and *sapiens* the species (the only extant species, all other species such as *neanderthalensis* and *erectus* now being extinct). 'Genus' and 'species' are the final elements of the taxonomy or classification of living creatures.

> 'I took these sketches in the second-class schoolroom… where about a hundred specimens of the genus *jeune fille* collected together offered a fertile variety of subject.'
>
> Charlotte Brontë, *The Professor*

Gratis

Free

In Umberto Eco's *The Name of the Rose*, William tells Adso that the boy's young peasant girl lover had given him '*gratis* and out of love' what would have cost others 'some ox heart and some bits of lung'.

Habeas corpus
Thou mayest have the body

Habeas is the second person singular present subjunctive of *habere*, 'to have', but has the effect of an imperative: 'You are to produce the body.' The phrase encapsulates the traditional (from the time of Magna Carta) British safeguard against wrongful detention, where the issue of a writ of *habeas corpus* [*ad subjuciendum*] requires the arresting authority to produce the prisoner before a judge, who will then decide whether the prisoner should remain in detention or be released.

Hic jacet
Here lies

The traditional first words for an inscription on a tombstone, eloquent in themselves.

'O, eloquent, just and mighty Death!… thou hast drawn together all the far-stretched greatness, all the pride, cruelty and ambition of man, and covered it all over with these two narrow words, *Hic jacet*.'

Sir Walter Raleigh, *A History of the World*

Hinc illae lacrimae
Hence those tears

This phrase comes from Terence, and also from Horace in *Epistles* 1:19:41.

> 'I am too much addicted to the study of philosophy; *hinc illae lacrymae*, sir, that's my misfortune. Too much learning hath been my ruin.'
>
> Henry Fielding, *Tom Jones*

Homo sapiens
Man who can think

This is the species to which all living men belong. Other phrases exist to describe subdivisions or various aspects of humanity, e.g. *Homo faber*, man the toolmaker, and *Homo erectus*, an earlier species of man, including Java man, able to walk upright. I myself, deprived once of the use of a car for several days, recognised my own sub-species as *Homo automobilis*.

A group of robotic toys is known as 'Robosapiens'.

Honorarium (donum)
An honorary gift

A fee of arbitrary size paid in acknowledgement of services given voluntarily, not always commensurate with the amount of work done.

Honoris causa
As an honour, a token of respect

Literally, 'for the sake of honour'.

In *What's The Joke?* Chaim Bermant suggests that God may not have claimed for Himself a sense of humour as a divine attribute, 'but it was, so to speak, conferred on Him, *honoris causa*, by the Jewish people'.

The phrase can denote the grounds for granting an honorary degree.

'In 1853 [Disraeli] went to Oxford to receive a doctor's degree, *honoris causa*.'

André Maurois, *Disraeli*

Horribile dictu
Horrible to relate

cf. mirabile dictu

<u>Mottoes of regiments</u>
<u>of the British Army:</u>

Invicta
Unconquered
Kent Volunteer Fencibles

Justitia turris nostra
Justice is our tower
The Hackney Territorials

Nemo me impune lacessit
No one gets away with mucking me about
The Black Watch

Pro aris et focis
For our altars and hearths
The Fife and Forfar Light Horse

Quis separabit
Who shall separate (us)?
The Sligo Rifles

Quo fata vocant
Whither the fates call
The Royal Northumberland Fusiliers

Semper fidelis
Always faithful
East Devon Militia

Vestigia nulla retrorsum
No steps backwards
5th (Princess Charlotte of Wales) Dragoon Guards

Hortus siccus
A dry garden, a herbarium

This could be my back lawn languishing under a hosepipe ban, but more particularly a *hortus siccus* is a collection of dried plants arranged in a book.

Humanum est errare
It is human to err

Seneca the Younger, in *Naturales Quaestiones* 4:2, merely repeats one of the most widely used of all Latin proverbs, which continues with *perseverare diabolicum* ('to persist is of the devil'). Alexander Pope extended its scope in a different direction in 'An Essay on Criticism', line 525: 'To err is human, to forgive, divine.'

In Giovanni Guareschi's *The Little World of Don Camillo*, Peppone admits his cardinal mistake in tying crackers to the church bells: '"It should have been half a ton of dynamite." "*Errare humanum est*," remarked Don Camillo.'

Ibidem (ibid., ib.)
In the same place

In, for instance, the *Oxford Book of Quotations*, the first quotation from a poem will be labelled with the name of the poem followed by the number of the line. Second and subsequent quotations from the same poem are then labelled simply 'ib.' with the new line number.

Idem (id.)
The same (person)

This word is used particularly in notes on sources or in bibliographies. Thus from the consecutive footnotes:

1. Raymond Thurman, *The Sources of Pleasure,* p. 39
2. *Idem, The Fact of Pain,* p. 192

we understand that Thurman was also the author of *The Fact of Pain*.

Id est (i.e.)
That is

'Père Simon, it seems, had closely watched me, had ascertained that I went by turns, and indiscriminately, to the three Protestant chapels in Villette – the French, German, and English – *id est*, the Presbyterian, Lutheran, Episcopalian.'

Charlotte Brontë, *Villette*

Iesus Hominum Salvator
Jesus the saviour of men

The letters IHS seen frequently on church furniture do not normally represent the initial letters of this phrase, but instead represent the first three letters of the name 'Jesus' in Greek: *iota, eta, sigma*.

Ignis fatuus
Will-o'-the-wisp, a foolish fancy

'Sir John Falstaff: When thou rann'st up Gadshill in the night to catch my horse, if I did not think thou hadst been an *ignis fatuus*, or a ball of wild fire, there's no purchase in money.'

William Shakespeare, *Henry IV Part 1* 3:3

Jonathan Keates, reviewing *Images of English* by R. W. Bailey in *The Observer*, referred to 'The *ignis fatuus* of feminist political correctness'.

Ignoramus
We do not know, we are ignorant

This is an ancient law term, written by a Grand Jury on the back of an indictment when they had decided that there was not enough evidence to justify a case proceeding to trial. The epithet was subsequently flung at anyone who doesn't know much.

Impedimenta
Encumbrances, impediments

The singular *impedimentum* is 'a hindrance'. The plural *impedimenta* referred to the baggage and essential supplies carried by an army, which slowed down its speed of advance and impeded its progress. The term is now firmly associated with holidaymakers' luggage.

Imprimatur
Let it be printed

So giving it the stamp of authority. In particular, a licence given by the Roman Catholic Church to print a book. A previous stage in the granting of such a licence is the *Nihil Obstat* ('Nothing hinders'), the finding by the censor of the diocese that the work is free of moral or doctrinal error. The *Imprimatur* indicates that the bishop or other ecclesiastical authority approves the book as well.

Sometimes the word is used as a guarantee of worth.

'Julie's initials at the bottom of any letter were the sure imprimatur of a clean and flawless sheet of typing.'

Colin Dexter, *Last Bus to Woodstock*

Imprimis

First (of all), for a start

'Grumio: Now I begin: *Imprimis*, we came down a foul hill...'

William Shakespeare, *The Taming of the Shrew* 4:1

Imprimis also marked the first component of a list.

vide item

In absentia

In one's absence

R. Bruce Lockhart, writing in *The Observer,* said: 'Higgs was sentenced to death *in absentia*, along with my father and Reilly.'

In articulo mortis

At the point of death, in the arms of death

'As to the youthful sufferer, he weathered each storm like a hero. Five times was that youth "in articulo mortis", and five times did he miraculously survive.'

Charlotte Brontë, *Villette*

In *Epistolae ad Quintum Fratrem* 5:19, Cicero says *in ipso articulo temporis* ('at this point in time'). Perhaps not surprisingly there appears to be no phrase in Latin for 'at this moment in time'.

In camera

In private, behind closed doors

A case heard in camera is heard in a closed courtroom or in a judge's private room, with outsiders excluded.

'Before the case started [the judge] told the jury part of it would be held *in camera* with press and public excluded.'

Report in *The Guardian*

The French have their own equivalent, *huis clos*, which is succinct and pithy: when a translation of Sartre's play of this name was mounted in London, it was presented under the title 'In Camera'.

In extenso

At length

'"We never report Sir Thomas *in extenso*. Only the fines and charges."'

Rudyard Kipling,
'The Village That Voted The Earth Was Flat'

'I shall... head it "No Copyright", so that other papers... may reproduce it *in extenso*... '

Julian Barnes, *Arthur and George*

In extremis

At the point of death, at one's last gasp

'... Addison died there, exhibiting his fortitude *in extremis* to [his stepson] the dissolute Earl of Warwick.'

E. V. Lucas, *A Wanderer in London*

Nowadays it is often used in a somewhat devalued sense to mean 'in extreme circumstances'. Katherine Whitehorn, reviewing a book on etiquette in *The Observer*, suggested that ordinary people needing advice would not spend money on such a book but would 'ask a friend or, in extremis, write to a magazine'.

In flagrante delicto
Caught in the act

Literally 'in flagrant villainy'. The Latin has the implication of a 'blazing crime' being committed at the time. In the past hundred years the phrase has come to imply no more than 'in the act of (illicit) love'. During that time most serious crimes – murder, arson, even rape – have become mentionable; only the misfortune of being detected in the heat of illicit love still attracts the euphemism 'in flagrante', as if there were no way elegant or delicate enough of putting it in the vernacular.

> 'Unfortunately for Kemp, however, Cedric Downes discovered the guilty pair *in flagrante delicto*, which as you will remember, Lewis, is the Latin for having your pants down.'
>
> Colin Dexter, *The Jewel that was Ours*

Infra
Below

In the visible spectrum of light, red and violet mark the extremities. Objects not hot enough to glow red emit invisible infra-red rays, rays 'below' the red section.

Also used by an author to denote 'further on' in the text.

cf. supra

Infra dignitatem (infra dig.)

Beneath (one's) dignity

'In Tyler's circle, he supposed, hotels were *infra dig.*, refuges for conventially minded people.'

Anita Brookner, *Incidents in the Rue Laugier*

In hoc signo (vinces)

By this sign (thou shalt conquer)

In hoc signo was the motto of Constantine the Great and the sign in question was that of the Cross, which Constantine saw in a vision before the Battle of Milvian Bridge in AD 312. *In hoc signo vinces* was also a phrase used by the Knights Templar and by the Freemasons.

In loco parentis
In place of a parent

One of the main drawbacks of schoolteaching is having to be constantly in the company of other people's children. Being *in loco parentis* one is entrusted with their care and is adjured to treat them as a loving parent would, but is usually quite glad to return them to the care of their true loving parent(s) at the end of the school day.

However, this quasi-parental role has now been replaced by the requirement that a teacher give such care as 'can be expected of a competent professional acting within the constraint of circumstances'.

In medias res
Into the thick of things

Horace used this phrase in *Ars Poetica* 148. He was irritated by Homer's habit of plunging the reader into the middle of a story, assuming that the reader already knows or can somehow divine telepathically what went before.

Writing of C. S. Lewis' novels in *The Guardian*, John Mullan said that at the start of *The Voyage of the Dawn Treader*, the three children found themselves simply plunged into the sea near King Caspian's ship. '*In medias res* is how most of the novels begin', with their characters hurried into a story that had already begun.

In memoriam
In memory of

Tennyson's poem 'In Memoriam', composed in memory of his friend Arthur Hallam, is one of the longest elegies in the language.

During the nineteenth century (when else?) the custom arose of sending 'In Memoriam' cards to friends and acquaintances, announcing the death of a family member.

In nomine Patris, et Filii, et Spiritus Sancti
In the name of the Father, and of the Son, and of the Holy Ghost

These words introduce the Ordinary of the Mass in the Roman Catholic Church.

In perpetuum
For ever

In propria persona
In his/her own person

Said of someone acting on his own behalf in person and not through a deputy or agent.

Inquisitio post mortem
An inquest

This phrase gave English the word 'inquest' as well as the phrase *post mortem* ('after death') for the clinical examination of a body. In the Middle Ages, however, an *inquisitio post mortem* was a judicial enquiry after the death of a prominent man or woman into the property owned by the deceased, into services owed to an overlord or to the Crown, and into who might be the rightful heirs to the deceased's property. A vast number of documents recording the results of such enquiries over many centuries are held in the National Records Office.

Insignia
Badges

Usually military badges, worn on the uniform. 'The Major was wearing the insignia of the Royal Corps of Signals.'

In situ
In place

Archaeologically speaking, an artefact is *in situ* if it has not been moved from the place where it was originally deposited.

Inter alia
Among other things

Joanna Slaughter, writing in *The Observer*, reported that over 4,000 members of the public had 'cried foul [on life insurance salesmen], claiming, *inter alia*, misrepresentation, breaches of polarisation, mis-selling, misleading literature and inappropriate advice'.

When applied to people rather than things, the neuter *alia* changes to the masculine *alios* or the feminine *alias*.

Interim
Meanwhile, in the meantime

Used now to mean simply a space of time between two events.

As an adjective it is equivalent to 'stopgap' or 'temporary'. In diplomatic circles a *chargé d'affaires ad interim* acts for an absent ambassador. An interim government or administration is usually more or less legitimate (*de jure* as well as de facto), and can be expected to give way before long to a permanent, properly constituted body.

In toto

In total, altogether

'He asked leave, therefore, to withdraw the charge *in toto…* '

Rudyard Kipling,
'The Village that Voted the Earth was Flat'

In transitu

In transit

The phrase 'in transit', now accepted as entirely English, is derived immediately from the Latin, the loss of the final 'u' going almost unnoticed.

In vinculis

Bound, in bondage

A *vinculum* is a bond, in particular the marriage bond: *a vinculo matrimonii* means 'from the bond of matrimony'. In mathematics, it is a horizontal line used in place of brackets: Newton used *vincula* rather than brackets in his mathematical writings. The fraction bar also acts as a *vinculum* in that sometimes when we remove a fraction bar, we must replace it with brackets.

A memorial to Sir Joseph Bazalgette stands in London on the Embankment which he built. It reads *Vincula flumini posuit,* which can be translated as 'He set bounds to the river'.

The Chapel Royal of St Peter ad Vinculis (St Peter in chains) is the parish church of the Tower of London.

In vino veritas
In wine, truth, that is,
drunken men speak the truth

We have Pliny's *Historia Naturalis* 2:14:141, to thank for this. Just to keep the record straight, we should note that the phrase is distilled from the longer one which Pliny actually wrote: *Volgoque veritas iam attributa vino est* ('Truth in the popular mind has come to be credited to wine').

In *Sweet Thursday*, John Steinbeck introduces Sonny Boy, the restaurateur whose martinis are guaranteed to loosen anyone's tongue: '*Veritas* is not only *in vino* but regularly batters its way out.'

> '*In vino veritas*, they say,
> Yet lying is so much the custom
> Of certain folk, the safest way
> Is, drunk or sober, not to trust 'em.'

anon.

In vitro
In a glass

In vitro fertilisation of the human egg is fertilisation outside the womb, leading to the birth of a 'test tube' baby. Generally, *in vitro* experiments are performed in a controlled environment using material removed from a living organism. Experiments made on parts of an organism which are still *in situ* are referred to as being *in vivo*, 'in a living (situation)'.

Ipso facto
By that (very) fact

'[He or she] is not a king or queen, because everything about such a person is *ipso facto* exceptional'.

Barbara Tuchmann, *A Distant Mirror*

Item
Also

This word was used originally to mark such components of a list as followed the first component. Subsequently it came to be used for the components (items) themselves.

> 'Olivia: … I will give out various schedules of my beauty; it shall be inventoried as, item, two lips, indifferent red; item, two grey eyes, with lids to them; item, one neck, one chin, and so forth… '
>
> William Shakespeare, *Twelfth Night* 1:5

Ius primae noctis
The right of the first night

The French *Droit de Seigneur* included the alleged right of the feudal lord to spend the first night of a vassal's marriage with the vassal's wife. Unfortunately for those to whose minds the story clearly has a certain appeal, there is apparently no firm evidence that such a practice ever existed.

The 'first night' need not be a nuptial one. In 'Two or Three Graces', Aldous Huxley observes that the sight of a free ticket always impresses simple mortals, who have no option but to pay for their pleasures: 'The critic's *jus primae noctis* seems to them an enviable thing.'

Labor omnia vincit
Work conquers all

This was the apt motto of Lord Attlee, Labour Prime Minister from 1945–51. It is also the motto of Ashton-under-Lyne, Bradford, Cheltenham College, the Royal Marsden Hospital and the State of Oklahoma.

Lapis lazuli
The lazulum stone

A bright blue feldspathoid mineral, often flecked or streaked with gold. The blue colour derives from constituent minerals such as lazurite, sodium aluminium silicate with some sulphur, while the flecks of gold indicate the presence of iron pyrites. The Late Latin word *lazulum* derives from the Persian 'lajward', the source also of the word 'azure'.

Lapsus linguae

A slip of the tongue

We may also have *lapsus calami* ('a slip of the pen'), and *lapsus memoriae* ('a slip of the memory'), these lapses being just as common in the young as in those in the clutches of *anno Domini*. Now that so many of us write no longer with a pen but with a computer keyboard, it seems legitimate to add *lapsus digitis* ('a slip of the finger') or *lapsus claviaturae* ('a slip of the keyboard') to the above list.

The Vatican has produced a lexicon of Latin words for modern artefacts and institutions, choosing *claviatura* for 'keyboard', both for piano and for the computer. The full list can be found in *Lexicon Recentis Latinitatis*, accessible through Wikipedia, 'Ecclesiastical Latin'.

Latet anguis in herba

A snake lurks in the grass

This comes from Virgil's *Eclogue* 3:93. We may safely assume the snake does not lurk for any benevolent purpose, hence the pejorative flavour of the phrase 'a snake in the grass'.

Laus Deo

Praise be to God

In Bourton-on-the-Water in Gloucestershire, above a doorway of an old building presumably with ecclesiastical connections in former times, these words appear as LAVS DEO. This doorway is now the entrance to public toilets.

Libra (£)

Pound

The literal meaning of *libra* is 'scales', and this is the name of the seventh sign of the zodiac. The name subsequently transferred to the weights used on the scales.

The £ which we now use as a symbol for the pound sterling is merely a capital L with one or two lines drawn across indicating that it is a unit of currency. Other currency symbols which have similar lines drawn across them are $ (dollars), ¢ (cents), € (euros) and ¥ (yen). In old documents using Roman numerals, £20 was written as xx^{li}, and even after the use of modern numerals had become the norm it was still common for £20 to be written as 20*l*.

It is clear that 'lb' denoting weight is a contraction of *libra*. A pound in money terms was originally the value of a pound (avoirdupois) of silver.

Lingua franca
A general language

A *lingua franca* comes into being to make commerce possible between peoples whose native tongues are mutually unintelligible. The phrase is only superficially Latin, being coined in medieval Italy as a label for a trade jargon used in the Levant, but it is included here because *lingua* was Latin for 'tongue'. *Franca* referred to the Franks, a German tribe who founded France, and whose name became a synonym among the peoples of the Near East for Western Europeans, such as the Crusaders.

Latin itself was a *lingua franca* among scholars throughout Europe from the founding of the first universities until well into the nineteenth century.

Litterae humaniores
Human letters or literature

This phrase has given us the term 'Humanities', as opposed to the 'sciences', in schools and colleges. (*Humaniores* is in fact 'more human'.)

Loco citato (loc. cit.)
In the place cited

In the course of writing, say, a magazine article, it may be necessary to quote from another article or book, giving the author, title, and page reference. A second reference to the same source can be given simply by mentioning the author's name followed by loc. cit. and the page number.

Locum (tenens)
A temporary replacement,
someone 'holding a place'

For most of us a locum is a doctor who stands in for our doctor when he or she is on holiday, but the term may occasionally be applied to a stand-in for a clergyman or for a member of any other profession. (The teaching profession still sticks with 'supply teacher'.)

Locus
A place

Not just a place, but a special place.

> The removal of newspaper offices 'from Fleet Street has given the Garrick [Club] new importance as a locus'.
>
> *The Observer*

Locus classicus
The stock example, the classic example

'Our *locus classicus* [of the "second wife" kind of affair]… was Sara Keays and Cecil Parkinson.'

Simon Hoggart, writing in *The Observer*

Locus standi
A place of standing, a recognised position

'It's bad for one's *locus standi* to live on a woman's charity.'

Iris Murdoch, *Under the Net*

Also the right to appeal before a court.

Lucifer
The light-bearer

Lucifer is the planet Venus when it is the morning star (as the evening star it becomes 'Hesper'). Also one of the names of Satan, acquired allegedly by a mistaken translation in Isaiah 15:12: 'How art thou fallen from heaven, O Lucifer, son of the morning!'

A 'lucifer' was a pre-safety match, referred to in the First World War song 'Pack up your troubles in your old kitbag… While you've a lucifer to light your fag, smile, boys, that's the style!'

Lux mundi
The light of the world

The light of the world manifests itself in a multitude of persons. But although we read in St Matthew's Gospel 5:14, *Vos estis lux mundi* ('Ye are the light of the world'), it is more usual to assign the title 'The Light of the World' to Christ himself since in John 8:12 we have: *Ego sum lux mundi* – 'I am the light of the world'.

Mottoes of the squadrons and branches of the RAF:

Corpus non animum muto

I change my body not my spirit

57 Squadron

Custodes urbis

Guardians of the city

903 County of London Balloon Squadron

E nocentibus innocentia

From harmful things, harmless things

5131 Bomb Disposal Squad

Experientia docet
Experience teaches
No. 6 Elementary Flying Training School

Non ignobiliter ancillari
To serve not ignobly as a handmaid
Dental Training Establishment RAF

Ubique loquimur
Everywhere we speak
No. 38 Group Tactical Communications Wing

Magna Carta
The Great Charter

Otherwise known as Magna Charta, this was obtained, some say extorted, by the barons from King John at Runnymede in 1215. Its aim was to shield the customary privileges and interests of the baronial class from attack by the Crown, the implication being that there was a law to which even the monarch was subject. Later the name came to embody the idea that everyone was entitled to the protection offered by the law of the land.

Addressing his fellow-jurors in the television episode of *Hancock's Half Hour* called 'Twelve Angry Men', Hancock famously asked, 'Does Magna Carta mean nothing to you? Did she die in vain?'

Magna cum laude
With great praise

This is slightly less praiseworthy than *summa cum laude* but definitely more praiseworthy than just plain *cum laude*.

Magnum
Large

Used chiefly in tandem with 'opus', but also used to indicate the particular size, traditionally two quarts, of a bottle of wine or spirits. It is most familiarly linked to champagne.

Magnum opus
A great work

'The writing… of this *Magnum Opus* had been going on as long as she could remember.'

Aldous Huxley, *Chrome Yellow*

Note that the plural of 'opus' (*q.v.*) is 'opera', which has its own special meaning in English writing and speech. The plural of *magnum opus* in Latin is *magna opera*, which is unwieldy; and so we can really do no better than to speak of *'magnum opuses'* in referring to more than one.

Mandamus
We command

A command issued by a higher court to a lower.

Manet

He remains

A stage direction opposed to *exit* ('he leaves') (*q.v.*).
The plural is *manent*.

Mare nostrum

Our sea

To the Romans the Mediterranean was 'Our Sea',
since the Roman Empire at its greatest extent included
all its coastline. When Italy entered the Second World
War in June 1940, Benito Mussolini claimed the
Mediterranean Sea for Italy under the title *Il Mare
Nostrum*. It was Gabriele D'Annunzio (1863–1938)
who had coined this revised phrase, giving it an
Italian definite article, in the course of urging the
development of the Italian Navy as an instrument of
Italian colonial expansion into Africa.

Mater

Mother

'Mater is not "frantic". Only the prospect of the
decanter running dry could make Mater frantic.'

David Mitchell, *Cloud Atlas*

M.B.
(Medicinae Baccalaureus)
Bachelor of Medicine

A Bachelor of Medicine is nonetheless entitled to call himself 'Doctor'. Clearly the word *Baccalaureus* gives the French their word *Baccalaureat*, which, however, is an educational qualification at a lower level than our Bachelor's degree.

M.D.
(Medicinae Doctor)
Doctor of Medicine

Mea culpa
Through my fault

This phrase comes in the Public Confession in the Mass, following the words *Peccavi nimis cogitatione, verbo, et opere* ('I have sinned exceedingly in thought, word and deed'). Then: *Mea culpa, mea culpa, mea maxima culpa* ('Through my fault, through my fault, through my most grievous fault').

Richard Brooks wrote in *The Observer* of a former government economic adviser who had suspicions that his advice in the past had helped to create unemployment: 'Budd's *mea culpa*, admirable in principle, may not go down so well with the jobless.'

> The negative of *mea culpa* is *mea non culpa* or 'Don't blame me!'
> 'Slater's *mea non culpa* was ghosted by an Australian rock journalist, Jeff Apter.'
>
> Gideon Haigh, *Silent Revolutions*

In *The Bell*, Iris Murdoch adapts the phrase to *felix culpa* ('joyous fault'): '… the joys of repentance… the delicious pleasure of… grovelling in the dust. *O felix culpa!*'

Media vita
in morte sumus

In the midst of life we are in death

This comes from the Book of Common Prayer and is part of the service for the burial of the dead, recited at the graveside.

Memento

A keepsake, a reminder

This is often misspelled 'momento', through a failure to associate it with the word 'memory'.

Memento hominem

Remember (thou art) a man

That is, mortal rather than immortal or divine. When a Roman General was enjoying his triumphal parade, he was accompanied by a slave whose duty it was to whisper in his ear from time to time, *Respice post te: hominem memento te* ('Look behind you: remember you're a man').

Memento mori

Remember you must die

A 'memento' is now simply a reminder, perhaps of a friend or of a holiday. A *memento mori*, a reminder of death, often took the form of a skull or skulls on the border of a memorial to a dead person.

Memento mori is the motto of the Trappists.

Mens sana in corpore sano

A sound mind in a sound body

This first appeared in Juvenal's *Satires* 8:356.

'This smiling, bespectacled icon… an advertisement for comradely physical improvement, *mens sana in corpore sano*.'

Julian Barnes, *Something to Declare*

In P. G. Wodehouse's *The Code of the Woosters*, Bertie Wooster felt that his 'sojurn… in the T-bath had done much to re-establish the *mens sana in corpore* what-not'.

Memorabilia

Things that are memorable, easy to remember

Used for things by which a person or object is remembered. A television game contestant was described as a 'collector of Winnie the Pooh memorabilia', and the collectors of railway memorabilia are legion.

Memorandum

(Something) to be remembered

Often shortened to 'memo'. The plural is 'memoranda'.

Minutiae

Details, the small print

cf. trivia

Mirabile dictu
Wonderful to relate

The phrase can be used to indicate surprise.

> 'In the first place, *mirabile dictu*, there were one or two even greater duffers than I on the Abbey cricket field.'
> E. W. Hornung, *Raffles*

The reverse side of the coin is *horribile dictu* ('terrible to relate').

Mobile vulgus
The common herd, the rabble

Or, in cut-down form, 'the mob'. Equivalent to the Greek *hoi polloi* ('the people'), but still a cut above *faex populi* (*q.v.*). *Vulgus* designates the common people, *mobile* implies that they are swift to shift their affections.

Modus operandi (M.O.)
The way of working

Inter alia, a well-known guide to the identification of a criminal, who betrays himself by the way in which he commits his crimes, although its use is not restricted to criminals.

'I sit at the piano… and we adopt one of our three *modi operandi*.'

David Mitchell, *Cloud Atlas*

Modus vivendi
A way of living (together)

Any two people who choose to live together have to arrive at a mutual accommodation which takes into account inevitable differences in personal taste and opinions. In short, they establish (with luck) a *modus vivendi*.

Anthony Burgess, writing in *The Observer*, suggests that Angus Wilson's novels 'are all about the need to construct a *modus vivendi* in a moral vacuum'.

Mons Veneris
The Mount of Venus

There are three Mounts of Venus on the human (female) body. Two are on the hands, at the base of each thumb; the third (and the one which probably most commonly springs to mind) is a fatty elevation on the pubic symphysis.

Multum in parvo
Much in a small space

The motto of Rutland, the smallest county in England (smallest except at high tide when the Isle of Wight is fractionally smaller).

Mutatis mutandis
With necessary changes

The writer of a letter in *The Guardian* quoted Kenneth Tynan's dictum that the function of theatre critics was to sell newspapers, not theatre tickets. 'The same applies, *mutatis mutandis*, to car reviewers.' Giles Smith's prose style was the attraction, not details of the car he was reviewing.

Nemine contradicente (nem. con.)
No one contradicting

Used in the House of Commons, and in any number of lesser gatherings, to signify that a vote was carried unanimously. The corresponding phrase in the House of Lords was/is *Nemine dissentiente (Nem. diss.)*, which means 'No one dissenting'.

Nemo me impune lacessit
None shall provoke me with impunity

This is the motto of the kings of Scotland and of all Scottish regiments. It is the motto of the Order of the Thistle, and also of the Nettles family, which if one thinks about it seems appropriate. The phrase is engraved around the edge of the Scottish pound coin, the coin itself bearing the impression of a thistle.

Ne plus ultra
No more, no further, the ultimate

Literally, 'no more beyond'. It can be argued that Marilyn Monroe was the *ne plus ultra* of twentieth-century pin-up girls.

Tradition has it that the twin Pillars of Hercules, situated at the Straits of Gibraltar and marking the westward boundary of the classical world, were joined by a scroll bearing the legend *Ne plus ultra* (or *Non plus ultra*). Such a device is currently found on the coat of arms of Spain. A Spanish silver dollar issued in 1563 displays the two pillars linked by such a scroll, and it is claimed that this design was simplified to give the familiar symbol for a dollar, $ with two vertical lines.

Nescit vox missa reverti
The published word can never be recalled

Literally, 'a voice sent forth knows not how to return'. Horace addressed his *Ars Poetica* 390 to Piso and his family, and is here advising Piso's eldest son to refrain from rushing too precipitously into print (or in those days, into manuscript).

In his edition of A. E. Housman's collected poems and selected prose, Christopher Ricks notes that in 1955 Tom Burns Haber published some of Housman's manuscript poems in violation of Housman's will and with a number of mistranscriptions. 'The dust… has since settled. And here too *Nescit vox missa reverti*… '

Nil desperandum
(Teucro duce et auspice Teucro)
We must not despair (with Teucer to
lead us and under Teucer's star)

Horace wrote this in *Odes* 1:7:27. Variants of the phrase such as *Nil carborundum* are of later date. During the Second World War, US General Joseph 'Vinegar Joe' Stilwell adopted as his motto *Illegitimis non carborundum*, translated loosely as 'Don't let the bastards grind you down'.

Nisi
Unless

Familiar from the (now obsolete) legal term 'decree nisi', implying that 'all will be well unless… '. In divorce cases this usually meant the party wanting the divorce in the first place had to behave properly and circumspectly for the next six months if the decree was to be made 'absolute'; once this was done, the new happy couple could get together and celebrate freely and in safety. It was in a way the opposite of a cooling-off period.

Nolens volens
Unwilling, willing

Whether he will or not, 'willy-nilly'.

Noli me tangere
Touch me not

'Jesus saith unto her [sc. Mary], Touch me not, for I am not yet ascended to my Father.'

John 20:17

The incident has been a popular one for paintings, such as that by Hans Holbein the Younger, now in Hampton Court, and that by Titian in the National Gallery.

The wild balsam plant has seed cases which when ripe and when touched spring open and scatter their seeds. A common name for the plant is 'Touch-me-not' and its botanical name is *Impatiens noli-tangere*.

Nolle prosequi
To be unwilling to continue

An indication by a plaintiff or by the public prosecutor in a court of law that for some reason he does not want to continue with his case against the defendant. A *locus classicus* was the case of Dr John Bodkin Adams (1899–1983) of Eastbourne, who in 1957 was accused of murdering two elderly patients (out of, some say, 163 *in toto*). He was found not guilty of the first case, whereupon the Attorney-General entered a controversial *nolle prosequi* for the second and seemingly stronger case. A *nolle prosequi* could also be won by plea-bargaining.

> "'[Waldo] stooled on a bank job… and got me four years. Got himself a nolle prosse.'"
>
> Raymond Chandler, 'Red Wind'

In P. G. Wodehouse's *Right Ho, Jeeves*, Jeeves rejected a suggestion by Bertie Wooster: "'… I am sorry, but I am afraid I must enter an unequivocal *nolle prosequi*.'"

Non Angli sed angeli
Not Angles but angels

According to tradition, probably based on an account of the incident in Bede's *History of the English Church and People*, these words were spoken AD *c*.600 by Pope Gregory I when told that the golden-haired young slaves in the market were Angles, that is, came from England. The incident happened before Gregory became Pope, but once he succeeded to the Papacy he began the task of converting Britain to Christianity.

Non compos mentis
Not of sound mind, mentally challenged

A legal term, hedged around with doubts about what constitutes sanity. Used by Cicero in *In Pisonem* 20:48.

In Aldous Huxley's *Antic Hay*, Mrs Viveash accuses Gumbril of clowning, but he declines to take any blame. If he were a clown then he 'was *non compos*, not entirely there, and couldn't be called to account for his actions'.

Non est inventus
He cannot be found

When a writ is served on a person and that person cannot be found, the phrase *Non est* (for *Non est inventus*) is or was written on the writ by the sheriff or bailiff.

Non est vivere, sed valere vita est
Life is not just being alive but being in health

This was written by Martial in *Epigrammata* 6:70.
Too true. It is the motto of the Royal
Society of Medicine.

Non sequitur
It does not follow

A non sequitur is a statement which does not seem to follow logically from anything that has been mentioned before.

Non sufficit orbis
The world is not enough

Juvenal wrote this in *Satires* 10:168. *The World is Not Enough* is the title of a James Bond film, and it so happens that *Non sufficit orbis* is the motto of the Bond family.

Nota bene (N.B.)

Note well

The Weekend Book published a culinary hint for those with a taste for exotic food: 'N.B. Mice in honey should be imported from China and not prepared at home.'

Nota Bene is the not inapposite name of innumerable choirs in Britain and in the United States and Canada.

Nulli secundus

Second to none

This is the motto of the Lombard Banking Company and of the Coldstream Guards. Placed as the second senior Regiment of Foot Guards in 1661, and they adopted this motto as a protest at being thus placed. They became the 'Coldstream Regiment of Foot Guards' in 1670.

Numero (no.)

In number

The abbreviation 'no.' is now used widely as an abbreviation of the word 'number' but the Latin provenance explains the 'o'.

Obiit

He (or she) died

To be seen on old tombstones and memorials, along with *Aetatis suae* and A.D., and often shortened to '*ob.*'.

Obiter dicta

Sayings by the way, comments in passing

Strictly speaking an *obiter dictum* was a comment made by a judge in court which was not to be counted as forming part of his judgment, an 'aside' as it were. *Dicta* is the plural of *dictum*.

A book review in the *Independent on Sunday* noted that James Wood had 'a trick of coining grand aphoristic *obiter dicta*' in a way that suggested he was the first writer ever to think of the idea.

Octavo
Eighth

A term used in printing, sometimes written '8vo', where a sheet of paper has been folded so as to make eight leaves of the book.

Odi et amo
I hate and I love

(Odi is technically the first person singular perfect tense of the verb, 'I have hated', but is used with a present tense meaning – 'I hate'.)

Catullus used the phrase in *Carmina* 85.

Odi et amo is the motto, for some undisclosed reason, of the family of Viscount Norwich. It is also part of the title of a series of television drama programmes, '*Odi et Amo* – Of Love and Hate', produced in Vancouver and dealing with the 'adult' themes of sadism and masochism.

Omnibus
For all

The 'bus' was designed 'for the use of all'. The original horse-drawn bus gave way in the twentieth century to the motor-bus, a name that prompted A. D. Godley's poem: 'What is this that roareth thus?/ Can it be a Motor Bus?/Yes, the smell and hideous hum/Indicat Motorem Bum… '

Opere citato (op. cit.)
In the work cited

In the course of writing, say, a magazine article, it may be necessary to quote from a book or other publication, giving the author, title and page reference. A second reference to the same book can be given simply by mentioning the author's name followed by 'op. cit.' and the page number.

Opus
Work

This term is used to cover the whole of the output of an artist or composer or other creative soul, and has its equivalent in the French term 'oeuvre'. On the other hand it is also used in the phrase 'opus number' as a label for a single piece of music. The plural of 'opus' is 'opera', which now has its own meaning in music. The masterpiece of an artist's output is his *magnum opus*.

Opus Dei
God's work

Opus Dei is a Catholic institution founded by Saint Josemaria Escrivá (1902–75). Its declared mission is to help people turn their work and daily activities into occasions for growing closer to God, for serving others and for improving society.

Oratio oblique
Indirect speech

Or reported speech – 'He said he was fed up' – as opposed to direct speech or *ipsissima verba* – '"I'm fed up!" he said.'

'…would it help to transfer the Ursula story into *oratio obliqua* for Kitty's benefit?' Philip Larkin, Notes for 'A New World Symphony'.

O tempora, o mores
O what times! O what conduct!

This was Cicero's reaction (in *In Catalinam* 1:1:1) to his suspicion that Catalina might be planning some sacrilegious crime. It could loosely be translated as 'Things ain't what they used to be'.

Writing in *The Guardian*, Tom Holland used these words in bemoaning the fact that the O.C.R. examination board had decided to abolish the A level papers in Ancient History.

Seaside Mottoes

Ilfracombe potens salubritate
Ilfracombe empowered by healthiness
Ilfracombe

Mare et ferro
By sea and steel
Redcar

Non sibi sed omnibus
Not for oneself but for all
Whitley Bay

Salus naufragis salus aegris
Safety to the shipwrecked, health to the sick
Ramsgate

Pabulum
Food, fodder

A somewhat derogatory but usually well-deserved label given to prepared food, such as traditional school meals. We referred in my school to a particular type of pudding as 'mattress'. Generations of children took consolation from the thought that the contents of their plates were nevertheless *pabulum* and, if nothing else, served to ward off starvation.

Pace (tua)
By leave of, with (your) permission

Pace is the ablative of *pax*; and *pace*, with or without the *tua*, is a polite but firm way of indicating dissent from someone else's views.

> 'Meanwhile, *pace* the tabloids, that other continuity prospers.'
>
> M. Church, writing in *The Observer*

Panem et circenses
Bread and circuses

Juvenal, in *Satires* 10:81, suggested that the two things the Roman populace most valued were free food and entertainment.

> '*Panem et circenses!* Only today education is one of the bad substitutes for a circus.'
>
> D. H. Lawrence, *Lady Chatterley's Lover*

[Both nouns are in the accusative case, which is fine if they are the object of the verb. The nominative is *panis et circenses*.]

Par
Level, equal

A term adopted in finance as well as in golf and in medicine – 'I'm feeling a little below par today'. It is a level with reference to which other achievements or situations are measured. 'This book is on a par with his previous works.' It is comparatively rare, however, to find anything categorised as 'above par'. In golf, of course, scoring below par is every player's aim.

Pari passu
With equal pace, together

'… his regret and himself were moving towards Arthur, or towards annihilation, *pari passu…* '
A. S. Byatt, *Angels and Insects*

Thomas de Quincey, considering murder as one of the fine arts, calls for an improvement in the style of criticism of masterpieces of murder. 'Practice and theory,' he says, 'must advance *pari passu.*'

Passim
Throughout

An indication that a particular subject is referred to in some passage of writing not once or twice but many times.

Pater
Father

Familiar to all readers of (public) school stories from the early part of the twentieth century as the usual word for referring to or addressing one's father: 'The pater won't be pleased when he hears about it.'

Paterfamilias

Father of a family

A 'Victorian paterfamilias' was traditionally one who kept his wife and children firmly under his thumb. Nevertheless, he might well have envied the powers of his Roman counterpart, the senior male member of a family, who could on a whim decide in the interests of eugenics or economy to condemn a new-born child to death by exposure and sell the survivors into slavery.

The species, although endangered, is not wholly extinct.

'Certainly there was Humphrey, who took on some kind of importance now as a latter-day paterfamilias.'

Anita Brookner, *Altered States*

Paternoster
Our Father

Pater noster are the first two words of The Lord's Prayer in Latin. Paternoster Row runs along the north side of St Paul's Cathedral.

Every eleventh bead on a rosary is a paternoster bead, at which point in telling the rosary the Lord's Prayer is repeated.

Sometimes the rosary itself is called a paternoster, and this practice gave rise to the naming of a fishing line with hooks and weights (and, with luck, fish) at intervals as a 'paternoster-line'. The name extends to other artefacts; a paternoster-wheel or paternoster-pump contains buckets on a chain, and the Bodleian Library's paternoster is a conveyor belt carrying books from the stacks to the main library and back.

Patria
Fatherland, homeland

Or, more to the British taste, 'motherland'. Essentially, the place one would like to return to for comfort and security, full of happy childhood memories, the next best place to the womb.

Pax
Peace

When I was at my grammar school, playground chases could be halted when exhaustion set in by the cry of *Pax* or *Paxes*. Only later did I realise that I was speaking Latin.

Pax Britannica
British peace

For a long time, between 27 BC and AD c.180, the Roman army, with the authority invested in them by the Senate and people of Rome, kept the *Pax Romana*, the Roman peace in the Empire, stamping down on rebellion and damping down internecine strife within its bounds. In the same way the British navy and army kept, with varying degrees of success, the *Pax Britannica* throughout the British Empire.

In a book review in *The Guardian*, Veronica Horwell mentions the *pax consumeria*, the peace which descends on the world when all potential combatants are busy shopping.

Per
By, each

Latin had no simple word for 'week', borrowing for the purpose the Greek *hebdomas*; hence, in addition to *per diem*, *per annum*, etc., we have by extension 'per week'.

'Per' also enables us to label rates succinctly: miles per hour (m.p.h.) is perhaps the most familiar example. It is an invitation mathematically to divide. Other examples are metres per second, miles per gallon, children per family, and words per minute (shorthand, typing or speech).

It will be remembered that the late Stanley Holloway told of how Mr and Mrs Ramsbotham and young Albert, their son, chose to walk across the Mersey at Runcorn rather than pay the exorbitant fare on the ferry. In reply to Albert's mother's indignation that the child should pay tuppence to cross the Mersey:

> '"Per tuppence per person per trip", answered Ted,
> "Per woman, per man or per child".'
>
> Marriott Edgar, 'The Runcorn Ferry'

It may crop up in places where it is used for emphasis, as in 'as per usual', or just following a whim, as in 'as per instructions'.

Per annum (p.a.)

Each year

Used almost exclusively to give a time scale to the charging of rates of interest. 'New low-cost mortgages at only 6.3% p.a.'

Per ardua ad astra

Through toil to the stars

The motto of the Royal Air Force, and before that of the Royal Flying Corps, possibly adapted from an early Latin tag, *Ad astra per aspera* ('To the stars through difficulties'), which itself is the motto of the State of Kansas.

Per capita

By heads, for each head or person

According to a leader in *The Guardian*, Finnish radio broadcasts the news in Latin to some 75,000 listeners, 'which on a per capita basis [of the total population] is… more than some BBC Radio 4 programmes get'.

Caput ('head'), of which *capita* is the plural, was used in Classical times to mean 'person'.

Per centum (per cent)
Out of 100

The symbol % is said by some to derive from the rearrangement of the digits of 100. It is also a reminder that, say, 12 per cent can be written for purposes of calculation as the fraction 12/100.

Per diem
Each day

Diem is the accusative of *dies*.

> '[The county laughed as Bob] abandoned the three-per-diem meals of the one-horse farm for the discontinuous quick lunch counters of the three-ringed metropolis.'
>
> O. Henry, 'The Defeat of the City'

Per mensem
Each month

Mensem is the accusative of *mensis*, whose plural is *menses*.

Per pro. (p.p.)
For and on behalf of

Used traditionally in offices when the person who wrote or dictated a letter is not available to sign it, in which case a secretary or other subordinate signs it 'p.p.' the author. Per pro. is also an abbreviation of per procurationem or 'through the agency of'.

Per se
On its own, by itself

Hugh Fearnley-Whittingstall writing in *The Observer* said: 'Robbins does not object to the flapjack *per se*.'

'Everything is symbolic. There is no such thing as a "thing" *per se*.'

Mervyn Peake, *Gormenghast*

Persona
Person

One's *persona* is the face we present to the long-suffering world at large, and one which may change with the company or the mood we are in. It was the name given to the mask worn by a Roman actor.

'[In *Cactus Flower*] Goldie Hawn converts her lovable *Laugh-In* kooky bimbo persona into a believable screen character.'

Radio Times film review

Persona grata
An acceptable person

A phrase technically used to confirm that a member of a diplomatic mission is acceptable to the country to which he is assigned. If for any reason, or for no reason at all, he is not acceptable, he is *persona non grata* (*q.v.*).

Persona non grata
An unacceptable person

'He [sc. Francis] and Celia would have to withdraw to Paris, *persona non grata* in London.'
Richard Condon, *Any God Will Do*

It was only Francis who was *persona non grata* in London, having been declared an undesirable alien following the unfortunate encounter with the belligerent dwarf. In Condon's sentence, it is not made clear which of the two was *non grata*. Had both been so, then the phrase would/should have appeared in the plural, *personae non gratae*.

Petitio principii
Begging the question, arguing in circles

This is not the same as 'asking the question' or 'raising the question', although it is often used in this sense by some voices in the media. Begging the question is more or less assuming as true a portion of what you are asked to prove, and adducing this as proof – stealing rather than begging. It can clearly lead to arguing in circles.

Placebo
I shall please

Used particularly of a medicine which makes you feel better, even though your G.P. may reckon it to have no inherent medical properties or curative powers.

Placens uxor
A pleasing wife, a sweet wife

Horace in *Odes* 2:14, mentions *domus et placens uxor* ('home and a pleasing wife') as two things one must leave when one dies.

Less tragically:

'The Colonel was not so depressed as some mortals would be, who, quitting a palace and a *placens uxor*, find themselves barred into a spunging-house…'

W. M. Thackeray, *Vanity Fair*

Plebs
A commoner

In ancient Rome, every free man was a *plebs* unless he was lucky enough to be a patrician or a knight. Now the word, together with its adjectival derivative, 'plebeian', is used in a pejorative sense to categorise one of the lower classes.

Posse
To be able

The *posse comitatus* ('available power') was the temporary police force of the locality which could be called out by the magistrates or by the sheriff when the need arose. The 'posse' survived longer perhaps in the American West than it did in its homeland of Great Britain.

In posse denotes possibility or potential.

'People are excited and regard every neutral as an enemy *in esse* or *in posse* [i.e. as an actual or potential enemy]'.

Ernest Bramah, 'The Secret of Headland Height'

Post-bellum
After the war

In the United States the post-bellum era is that following the Civil War of 1861–5.

Post coitum
After coitus

In Aldous Huxley's *Point Counter Point*, Philip Quarles states that books and lectures drown sorrows better 'than drink and fornication; they leave no headache, none of that despairing *post coitum triste* feeling'.

Aristotle, '*Quod omne animal post coitum est triste.*' (Every animal is sad after coitus.)

Post facto
Afterwards, after the act

Literally 'after (something has been) done'.

Post hoc, ergo propter hoc
After this, therefore because of this

Quoted by Richard Whately in *Elements of Logic* (1826), this well-known logical fallacy suggests that if two things happen at different times, the earlier must be the cause of the later.

In the debate about whether or not the MMR vaccine can cause personality disorders in some children, opponents of the vaccine claim that many children show symptoms of such disorders after they have been vaccinated. Defenders of the vaccine claim that there is no firm evidence that it is harmful, and suggest that those who claim it is harmful are arguing fallaciously along *Post hoc, ergo propter hoc* lines.

Post meridiem (p.m.)
After noon, after midday

Post mortem
After death

A 'post mortem' examination is usually carried out to ascertain the cause of death. In earlier times, an *inquisitio post mortem* (*q.v.*), which gave us the word 'inquest', was an inquiry into the dead man's holdings of land and the duties of service attached thereto.

The phrase can be used adverbially, as in 'The thumbs must have been cut off *post mortem* as there was no sign of extensive bleeding.'

The phrase has two possible plural forms.

> '"Nothing we can do till we get some reports, results of the post-mortems – "
> "Somebody once told me the plural should be post-mortes."
> "Bloody pedant!"
> "It was you actually, Morse."
> Colin Dexter, *The Remorseful Day*

Postscriptum (PS)
Written after, a postscript

And hence PPS for *post-postscriptum*.

> 'A considerable length of time separates the ending of my journal proper and this *postscriptum*.'
> William Golding, *Close Quarters*

Praemonitus, praemunitus

Forewarned is forearmed

This is the motto of the Intelligence
School of the RAF.

Prima facie
At first sight

Often translated as 'on the face of it', and having
regard to the evidence so far available.

Primus inter pares
First among equals

In *Silent Revolutions*, Gideon Haigh comments that the people of New South Wales 'have always regarded themselves as *primus inter pares*, reflected in the car number plates,' which still bear the inscription 'The Premier State'.

The term *primus inter pares* was used to mollify those members of the Roman Senate who considered the Emperor to be too powerful, and was intended to suggest that he was really just one of the boys. In more recent times the phrase has been used to define the status of the British Prime Minister in relation to his colleagues. It can in fact be applied to the nominal heads of many organisations, implying that they may at any time be eased from office and replaced by others equally well qualified to carry out the duties of the post.

Pro bono publico

For the public good

Two prolific writers of letters to the newspapers have been 'Disgusted of Tunbridge Wells', and 'Pro Bono Publico'. The latter writes disinterestedly, merely putting into words the thoughts of less articulate fellow members of the public.

Pro bono, used by lawyers and other professionals, can also mean 'free of charge'.

> 'The Tax Advice for Older People project provides pro-bono advice... for low-income earning older people.'
>
> *The Guardian*

Pro bono omnium ('For the good of all') is the motto of Guinness Mahon Holdings, Ltd.

Pro forma

As a matter of form

In government circles certain problems have always cropped up frequently, and traditional ways have been devised of dealing with them. Often a standard letter will suffice, *mutatis mutandis*, to deal with several related problems, the reply being in a standard form; in short, a reply *pro forma*.

In reply to requests for interviews from national newspapers across the continent, says David Mitchell in *Cloud Atlas*, 'I have the pleasure of despatching a polite but firm *pro forma* rejection to each'.

The organisation in question might need information from several different sources and would then send out copies of a schedule to be completed with spaces for replies, known simply as a 'pro forma'. In the late 1940s I worked for a disastrous fortnight in an RAF squadron office, and the Flight Sergeant in charge was always asking me to send out 'pro formas' to be filled in. Now my successor will simply be sending out 'forms' to be filled in (or more probably – *O tempora!* – to be filled 'out'). It seems probable that this word 'form' is itself a rendering into English of *pro forma*.

Propaganda (fide)
For spreading (the faith)

According to *Chambers Dictionary*, a congregation of the Roman Catholic Church formed by Pope Gregory XV in 1622 was charged with spreading the Catholic faith. The phrase used – *de propaganda fide* – ('concerning the faith to be propagated') – has given us the word 'propaganda'. This word has by now acquired a thoroughly pejorative flavour, so that 'propaganda' is seen to be composed, if not of blatant lies, then of statements which are to be taken *cum grano salis*.

Pro patria
For (one's) country

This phrase is inscribed on many war memorials, including the memorial erected on the Battery Rocks in Penzance. It is also the motto of the Royal Canadian Regiment.

vide dulce et decorum est

Pro rata

In proportion

Literally the phrase means 'by calculation' and all calculations made *pro rata* will be exact. It was early on connected with taxation and inheritance, dividing up the spoils fairly or otherwise. A part-time worker paid *pro rata* will receive a fixed proportion of the full-time wage, based on how many hours are worked.

'The cost of hiring a boat is £12 per hour, with parts of an hour being charged *pro rata*.' From this we can calculate that the charge for 1½ hours will be £18 while that for ¾ hour will be £9.

Pro re nata

Invented (born) for the purpose

Sometimes action needs to be taken to cope with an emergency, and special rules of action are devised for the occasion, that is, *pro re nata*. On medical prescriptions this is abbreviated to 'p.r.n.' and means (take) 'when an emergency arises', i.e. when you feel poorly.

The Free Church of Scotland constitution makes provision for *pro re nata* meetings designed to deal with unforeseen situations which require urgent action.

'He invented rule and reference *pro re nata…* '
    Rudyard Kipling, 'The Pit That They Digged'

Pros and cons
Pros and contras, arguments for and against

Prosit tibi
May it go well with thee

Prosit is still used as a toast, especially in Germany, pronounced as if the 'i' were absent.

In *Women in Love*, D. H. Lawrence describes 'an excited clamour of voices, a chinking of mug-lids, a great crying of "Prosit – Prosit!"'

Pro tanto
For so much, to that extent

'Every change is a shock; every shock is a *pro tanto* death.'

Samuel Butler, *The Way of All Flesh*

Pro tempore (pro tem)
For the time being

'The services of Mr William Terence Keogh as acting consul, *pro tem.*, were suggested and accepted.'

O. Henry, *Cabbages and Kings*

A young lady who came in once a week during the 1939–45 war to help my mother keep our house clean used to explain that she was only working in this way 'pro tem' until such time as her husband returned from the war.

Proviso
A (legal) condition

The full Latin term is *proviso quod* ('it being provided that').

Proxime accessit
Came second, next, close

Used in the ancient universities to indicate on lists of prizewinners those who didn't quite come first.

Pudenda

(Bodily parts) to be ashamed of

These are the bits below the waist about which Adam and Eve became self-conscious following the unfortunate incident of the apple, and to hide which they wore fig-leaves. In these more enlightened days, we are perhaps less ashamed of them.

The pudenda include A. P. Herbert's 'portions of a woman that appeal to man's depravity', to which doctors have given 'delightful Latin names'. Most of these names started off life as euphemisms. The vagina, for instance, is a sheath: every good blade should have one.

Men also possess pudenda.

'The body... without hair, seemed a woman's except for the obscene spectacle of the flaccid *pudenda*.'

Umberto Eco, *The Name of the Rose*

Mottoes of Waterworks

Before privatisation, water working was often a very
dignified business, judging by its mottoes.

E rupe erumpit aqua
From the rock shall break forth water
Grimsby, Cleethorpes and District Water Board

Et plui super unam civitatem
And I cause it to rain upon one city
Metropolitan Water Board

Nil sine aqua
Nothing without water

South Staffordshire Waterworks Co.

Semper praebebimus
We'll always supply
Newport and Monmouthshire Water Board

Qua
As, simply as

In *Aspects of the Novel*, E. M. Forster writes: 'And now the story can be defined… *Qua* story, it can only have one merit', which is to make the audience want to know what happens next.

Quaestio
I ask

Not used in English writing very much, if at all, but interesting because it gave us a punctuation mark, *viz* the question mark '?', formed originally from the first and last letters of *quaestio* set one upon the other.

Quarto
Fourth

The size of page obtained when a sheet of paper has been folded so as to make four leaves of a book; written '4to' for short. The name is applied also to a book composed of sheets folded in this way.

Quasi
As if, like

A 'quango' is a Quasi-Autonomous Non-Governmental Organisation. A quasi-historical novel is based only loosely on such historical facts as are known for (more or less) certain.

Qui desiderat pacem, praeparet bellum
Whoever seeks for peace,
let him prepare for war

This was said by Flavius Vegetius Renatus, *De Rei Militari* c.390 BC.

Quid nunc
What now?

A gossip, always asking after the latest scandal. (In Latin the two words are separate: *Quid nunc*?)

Quid pro quo
Something more or less equivalent in return

F. P. Smoler, writing in *The Observer*, mentions 'the gangster Frank Costello, with whom (J. Edgar) Hoover had a notorious *quid pro quo*', a mutual understanding of give and take.

The technically correct plural of *quid pro quo* is either *qua pro quo* or *quae pro quo*, but it seems sensible to follow the example of such writers as Ivor Brown who, in *Chosen Words*, mentioned *quids pro quo*. This is certainly far preferable to *quid pro quos*.

Quietus (est)

He is quiet

In medieval Latin this came to mean 'he is quit', which is to say someone has discharged all his or her debts and is free to go. In *The Duchess of Malfi* the Duchess tells her newly-acquired husband, Antonio, her former steward:

> "'I thank you, gentle love:
> And 'cause you shall not come to me in debt,
> Being now my steward, here upon your lips
> I sign your *Quietus est*.'"

For others, one's *quietus* is one's end, when all debts are finally paid.

> 'Then I turned to see how Good had fared with the big bull, which I had heard screaming with rage and pain as I gave mine his quietus.'
>
> H. Rider Haggard, *King Solomon's Mines*

Quod erat demonstrandum (QED)
Which was to be demonstrated

It was originally Euclid who said this.

> 'So, the matter was clear: one, the shoes in the cabin belonged to Joanna Franks; two, the shoes had been worn by the drowned woman; therefore, three, the drowned woman was Joanna Franks – QED.'
>
> Colin Dexter, *The Wench is Dead*

Quod vide (q.v.)
Which see

This is an invitation to look at something. If there is more than one thing the writer would like you to see, he will use 'qq.v.'.

Quondam
Formerly

More often used as an adjective to mean 'former'.

> 'Robert Adley, M.P., spoke out against his quondam guru [Viscountess Thatcher] and called her ladyship "a former Finchley fishwife".'
>
> Pendennis, *The Guardian*

Quorum
Of whom

The word appeared originally in the invitation written in Latin to a person to join the local bench of justices of the peace, 'of whom we will that you be one... '. It was used subsequently in connection with the number of justices of the peace who had to be present in court before business could begin; and thence as a term for the magistracy itself.

Now used to indicate the number of members of any committee or suchlike body who must be present before business may commence.

Quota
A share

A useful term based on the Latin *quot* ('how many?') and familiar from its use in deciding how much fish, milk, etc., a particular person or organisation may catch, produce or market.

Quot homines,
tot sententiae

However many men, so many opinions

First said by Terence in *Phormio* 454.

On 8 June 2005 Hansard reports that Sir Menzies Campbell commented in the House of Commons on the apparent multiplicity of opinions on the Opposition benches: 'I know that it is advised that Latin be used sparingly in the House, but I cannot help saying, *"Quot homines, tot sententiae".'*

Rara avis in terris,
nigroque similima cycno

A rare bird on earth, like a black swan

When Juvenal wrote this in *Satires* 6:165, he knew nothing of the black swans of Australia: his was a just simile. The reference was to a chaste and faithful wife. To be fair, he said that a good man is a rare animal too: *Vir bonum est animal rarum.*

Rara Avis is the name of a rainforest reserve in Costa Rica. Jeremy Sams, writing in *The Independent*, said of Lorenzo the Magnificent that 'he was after all, that *rara avis*, a Jewish Catholic priest with a wife and children'.

Re
Concerning

Recipe
Take

The medical profession has traditionally written prescriptions wholly or partly in Latin. At a period when pharmacists made up their own pills and powders, the prescription would begin 'Recipe… ' followed by a list of ingredients, *recipe* being the imperative of *recipere*, 'to take'. The writers of early cookery books copied the formula – 'Recipe ½lb of flour, etc.' – and the word 'recipe' moved over without fuss from the consulting room to the kitchen.

Reductio ad absurdum
Reduction to the absurd

A method of proof which begins by making assumptions and which follows the logical implications of those assumptions to an absurd conclusion, thereby showing that one or more of the original assumptions must be false.

Nowadays the phrase is used to highlight any absurdity. In an *Observer* article on the question of abortion in Ireland, Emily Bell quoted *The Irish Times* as describing the sequence of events as 'just the latest *reductio ad absurdum* in the theatre of the absurd of Irish public life'.

Referendum
To be referred to

A referendum is a call to the people to give their opinion on a particular question – a question 'to be referred to' the people. The plural of referendum is *referenda*, but this would suggest that more than one question is asked, rather than that more than one referendum is to be issued. In the latter case, we have to accept the plural 'referendums'.

Regalia
The insignia of royalty

Originally these could also be the powers attached to the throne, but now the term applies only to visible symbols of majesty – the crown, the sceptre, the orb, the sword of state, etc. Other organisations also have their regalia.

Regina
The Queen

In criminal cases brought to court by the Director of Public Prosecutions, the Crown Prosecution Service acts in the name of the Queen, and so each such case is referred to as *Regina versus* the accused. At times when the monarch happens to be a king, then the case is *Rex versus* the accused.

Requiem
Rest

The first word of the Requiem Mass, the Mass for the Dead. The full line is *Requiem aeternam dona eis, Domine, et lux perpetua luceat eis* ('Grant them, O Lord, eternal rest, and may light perpetual shine upon them').

Requiescat in pace
(R.I.P.)
May he/she rest in peace

'R.I.P.' is a familiar inscription on tombstones and memorial tablets.

Resurgam
I shall rise again

This terse epitaph inscribed on a gravestone was popular in the sixteenth and seventeenth centuries, but later became less popular.

Resurgam is said to have been found engraved on a lump of stone excavated from the ruins of Old St Paul's, destroyed in the Great Fire of London, 1666, carrying promise of the successful rebuilding of the cathedral.

Resurgam was the name of the first mechanically-powered (steam-driven) British submarine, designed and built by Rev. George Garrett in 1879. The name reflected her builder's confidence in her seaworthiness, and her trials proved successful, although she was lost at sea when under tow in 1880.

Rigor mortis

A stiffening of the body in death

Apparently not only in death but occasionally in life also, since 'Rigor Mortis' was the nickname given to a particularly unbending nurse in Richard Gordon's *Doctor in the House*.

Ian Buruma, writing in *The Guardian*, suggests that making a utensil as a pure work of art 'can lead to decadence, when the stylised performance hardens into a kind of aesthetic *rigor mortis*'.

Rostrum

A beak, a prow

A pulpit or platform, such as that in the Forum in Rome from which orators addressed the public, and which was decorated with the prows of ships.

Sanctum sanctorum
Holy of holies

According to *Brewer's Dictionary of Phrase and Fable*, the *Sanctum sanctorum* was the 'Holy of Holies in the Jewish Temple, a small chamber into which none but the high priest might enter… '. It is applied to any place, physical or metaphorical, where a man or woman may be safe from intrusion.

> 'Mdlle. Reuter turned her eye laterally upon me, to ascertain, probably, whether I was collected enough to be ushered into her *sanctum sanctorum*.'
>
> Charlotte Brontë, *The Professor*

Jonathan Keates, writing in *The Observer*, cited a writer's 'essay on football, that *sanctum sanctorum* of British maleness… '.

Scilicet (sc.)
Namely, to wit

This is one of a number of expressions (*cf.* I.E., VIZ.) used to specify who or what we are talking about. 'Scilicet' tends to refer to someone we have already mentioned but whose identity is not clear from the context.

Semper eadem

Always the same

The motto of Queen Elizabeth I and of later English queens, and only of queens, since *eadem* is feminine. However, families, cities and schools are also feminine and it is the motto of the City of Leicester, Elizabeth College, Guernsey, and Ipswich School.

Semper fidelis

Ever faithful

This is the motto of the East Devon Militia, the City of Exeter, the Plymouth Argyle Football Club and the Reliance Mutual Life Assurance Society.

Sic
In this way, in this manner, thus

Used to make it clear that whatever is printed is someone else's responsibility, or that, believe it or not, this is the truth.

'In his letter he wrote: "The new regulations have not superceded [*sic*] the old regulations but have clarified them".' *Sic* here means: 'Have no fear; I know how to spell "superseded" even if he doesn't.'

Sic transit gloria mundi
Thus passes the glory of the world

This is attributed to Thomas À Kempis in *De Imitatione Christi* (Of the Imitation of Christ). In fact, he wrote: *O quam cito transit gloria mundi* ('O how swiftly passes… '). The phrase *Sic transit…* derives from this and is used at the enthronement of a new pope. Three times a monk interrupts the ceremony, holding a piece of burning flax on a pole and saying *Sic transit gloria mundi* as the flax burns away.

> 'Outside the railings, the hollow square of crumbling houses, shells of a bygone gentry, leaned as if in ghostly gossip over the forgotten doings of the vanished quality. *Sic transit gloria urbis.*'
>
> O. Henry, 'Proof of the Pudding'

cf. memento hominem

Sine die
Without a day (being fixed)

When a law sitting or other gathering is adjourned *sine die*, it means that it has finished its business and almost certainly will never be reconvened.

Sine qua non
Without which nothing (happens)

Short for *causa* (or *conditio*) *sine qua non*.

A government farming expert, speaking on the radio about grassland, once famously remarked that a *sine qua non* of a good ley was a firm bottom.

Solidus (s.)
Shilling

The solidus was a Roman coin which gave its name in the Middle Ages to the British shilling; British 'pounds, shillings and pence' were indicated by the letters '£ s. d.' which stood for 'librae, solidi, denarii'. The 's.' of 'solidi' became lengthened. So 20s. was written for much of the time as 20/-, and 2s. 6d. was written as 2/6. The 'long s' is still in use today as a 'forward slash' or a fraction bar – we write 3/7 for 'three sevenths' – and the technical term for this symbol is still 'solidus'.

'Solidi' were used to pay fighting men in an army, who are consequently still known as 'soldiers'.

Solvitur ambulando
It is solved by walking

That is, by observation and by poking one's nose into things, rather than by sitting and cogitating.

Species
Species

This is the singular form in Latin, so we must talk about a species and not about a specie. The word 'specie', from the Latin in specie ('in actual form'), is used now to refer only to coined money – 'real' money as opposed to the flimsy paper variety.

Splendide mendax
Splendidly false, or Nobly untruthful

When Horace wrote this in *Odes* 3:11:35, he was heaping praise on Hypermnestra, one of the fifty daughters of Danaus. Danaus had instructed each of his daughters to kill her husband on their wedding night, but Hypermnestra refused, breaking her promise to her father and warning her husband to flee for his life. The phrase *splendide mendax* has appealed to writers ever since, particularly to applaud the use of feminine wiles when these are employed for humanitarian ends.

Splendide mendax is the *locus classicus* of an oxymoron.

Status quo (ante)
Previous state, situation

Time is, as it were, of the essence when we come to use this phrase. When we seek to maintain the *status quo* we are seeking to preserve our present state in the face of an imminent threat to alter it; we mean to keep it exactly as it was a moment ago. On the other hand, in seeking to restore the *status quo* we may be looking at a state of affairs at any point in the near or distant past.

'The exact mind which of all others dislikes the stupid adherence to the *status quo*, is the keen, quiet, improving Whig mind… '
Walter Bagehot, 'The First Edinburgh Reviewers'

Stella maris
Star of the sea

This title is often given to the Blessed Virgin Mary.

Stet
Let it stand

Used by an editor when he or she has second thoughts about altering a section of copy, reversing his original decision to change or delete it.

Sub judice
Under consideration by the courts

Severe restrictions exist on the reporting or discussion in print of any matter which is *sub judice*, for fear of a jury being influenced by anything except the evidence properly presented to them in court.

Sub poena
Under penalty (if you do not turn up)

This is the origin of the verb 'to subpoena' and of the phrase 'to issue a subpoena', whereby a witness is required to appear in court at a particular time, and stands liable to some penalty if he or she fails to turn up.

As part of the attempt to remove Latin from the proceedings in English and Welsh civil courts, the phrase 'witness summons' has recently replaced the noun 'subpoena'.

Sub rosa

Under the rose

That is, confidentially or secretly. Charles Lamb uses the English version in 'Mrs Battle's Opinions on Whist': '... I have heard her declare, under the rose, that Hearts was her favourite suit.'

Richard Condon, two hundred years on from Lamb, in *The Final Addiction*, uses the Latin, in relating how Osgood Noon ascended the ladder of promotion slowly, 'starting as Deputy Director of the Kansas Bureau of Fisheries, a *sub-rosa* CIA post... '.

Thomas Browne tells us in *Pseudodoxia* that the rose was the flower of Venus and was dedicated to Harpocrates, the god of Silence, as a bribe to persuade the latter not to reveal details of Venus' love life. The phrase *sub rosa* is said to arise from the custom of a host at dinner hanging a rose above the table as an assurance that anything said at the table would be treated by all present as a matter of the strictest confidence.

Sui generis
Of its own kind, 'one of a kind'

Writing of Angus Wilson's *The Old Men at the Zoo* in *The Observer*, Anthony Burgess said: 'The genre was unclear… but is now perhaps seen as *sui generis*… '

Summa cum laude
With highest praise

Used particularly to denote the award in the United States of a university degree of the highest class, more or less equivalent to a British first class degree. Below this class is *magna cum laude* ('with great praise'), and below this is plain *cum laude*.

Sunt lacrimae rerum et mentem mortalia tangunt

*Tears abound in all things and human
suffering touches the heart*

This was Aeneas' anguished cry (in Virgil's *Aeneid*
1:462) when he saw scenes of the battles of Troy
depicted in carvings on the walls of the temple in
Carthage, his grief brought on particularly by the
image of King Priam.

In David Mitchell's *Cloud Atlas*, Robert Frobisher's
suicide note concludes with the words *Sunt lacrimæ
rerum*, while the entire quotation furnishes a heading
to chapter 34 in Colin Dexter's *The Remorseful Day*.

Supera moras

Overcome delays

This is the motto of Bolton Wanderers Football Club.

Superbia in proelio

Pride in battle

This is the motto of Manchester City Football Club.

Suppressio veri suggestio falsi (est)

Suppression of the truth implies a falsehood

There seems to have been little need to coin the phrase 'economical with the truth'. This maxim has the force of law behind it. Insurance companies in particular require their policy-holders to reveal all relevant facts when applying for cover.

Supra

Above

Vide supra is an invitation to look for a reference in earlier pages of a book or article.

Tabula rasa
A clean slate

Often used to refer to the human brain before it becomes cluttered with information.

The Laurel and Hardy fan club has the motto *Duae tabulae rasae in quibus nihil scriptum est* ('Two clean slates on which nothing has been written' or 'Two minds without a single thought').

Taedium vitae
Boredom, the tedium of living

'The notion of liberty amuses the people of England, and helps to keep off the *taedium vitae.*'
James Boswell, *The Life of Samuel Johnson, LL.D*

In *The Picture of Dorian Gray*, Oscar Wilde decribes the hero of a novel as being 'sick with that *ennui*, that terrible *taedium vitae*, that comes on those to whom life denies nothing'.

Tandem
At length

The English use of this word is a pun upon the Latin. The *OED* gives a late eighteenth-century example of its use, from Grose's *Dictionary of the Vulgar Tongue*: 'Tandem – a two-wheeled chaise, buggy or noddy, drawn by two horses, one before the other, that is *at length*.' If three horses were in harness in this way, the arrangement was known as random-tandem.

The tandem bicycle, on which two people sit one behind the other, came on the scene *c.*1884. Because a tandem is a bicycle made for two, 'in tandem with' is occasionally used to mean 'alongside' or 'in conjunction with'.

Writing in *The Guardian*, Sue Arnold suggests: 'You should probably listen to this collection [of Shakespeare extracts] in tandem with the same plays broadcast on Radio 3 over the past five years… ' However, two things are in tandem if one is in front of the other. If she means 'first one version, then the other', then 'tandem' is appropriate. If not, then 'in parallel with' might be a better phrase to use.

Tempora mutantur nos et mutamur in illis

Times change, and we too change along with them

This phrase first appeared in *Proverbalia Dicteria* published by A. Gartneus in 1566, but is credited earlier to Lothair I, who was Holy Roman Emperor AD *c.*850.

'Poor James… such curly hair he had then… *nos et mutamur.*'

Aldous Huxley, *Eyeless in Gaza*

Tempus edax rerum

Time the devourer of things

Ovid wrote this in *Metamorphoses* 15:234.

'"Mr Western a daughter grown up!" cries the barber. "I remember the father a boy; well, *tempus edax rerum!*"'

Henry Fielding, *Tom Jones*

Tempus fugit
Time flies (or flees)

This distils the essence from *Sed fugit interea, fugit inreparabile tempus* ('Time is fleeing, fleeing beyond recall').

Virgil, Georgics 3:284

Terminus
Limit, end point

In the 1830s *terminus* (plural *termini*) was adopted for the place where the railway tracks ended (or began).

A *terminus ad quem* is a 'finishing point'. Michael Hofmann, writing in *The Guardian*, said: 'It [sc. the history of Germany] comes inevitably down to Hitler, the *terminus ad quem*.' Conversely, *terminus a quo* is a 'starting point'.

These two terms are also used in a slightly different context to mark the limits of the time at which an event could have taken place. For example, a borough charter for Looe in Cornwall is known to have been drawn up in the early years of the thirteenth century. The earliest possible date for the charter, the *terminus a quo*, is 1212, the date at which one witness inherited his estate and title. The latest possible date, the *terminus ad quem*, is 1229, the date at which another witness is known to have died.

Terra firma
Firm ground

Martin Amis in *The Information* quotes an air hostess looking for a passenger. "'A Mr Tull at all?'" He labels the question as 'airspeak; no one on *terra firma* would ever talk like that'.

Terra incognita
The Unknown Land

A name given most commonly to Antarctica, the last of the unexplored regions of the earth.

Samuel Taylor Coleridge, in his notes on Shakespeare's *Richard II,* writes in a non-geographical sense of 'Shakespeare's gentleness in touching the tender superstitions, the *terrae incognitae* of presentiments, in the human mind... '.

Thesaurus
Treasure

Roget's *Thesaurus of English Words and Phrases* contains the language's verbal treasure. The word originally was Greek, but was assimilated into Latin, and from thence gave us in time our own word 'treasure'.

Timeo Danaos et dona ferentes

I fear the Greeks, even when they come bearing gifts

This comes from Virgil's *Aeneid* 2:48. The gift in question was the wooden horse left outside the gates of Troy, and the speaker is Laocoon, voicing his misgivings at the sight of it.

> '… on the principle of *"timeo Danaos"* etc., I instantly smelt a ruse…'
>
> Erskine Childers, *The Riddle of the Sands*

> 'Tell Mrs Boswell that I shall taste her marmalade cautiously at first. *Timeo Danaos et dona ferentes.* Beware… of a reconciled enemy.'
>
> James Boswell, *The Life of Samuel Johnson, LL.D*

The 216 (Bomber Transport) squadron of the RAF has the motto *CCXVI dona ferens* ('216 bringing gifts').

Trivia
Trifles

Trivia are details, but unlike *minutiae* which are significant details, *trivia* are unimportant details, too trivial to appear even in the small print. At the time of writing, the *Radio Times* contains a regular column entitled 'Film Trivia', a collection of unimportant though not uninteresting stories connected with the making of well-known films.

Black Metal Bands

The website *Encyclopaedia Metallum* lists some 56,000 Black Metal bands worldwide, of which several hundred have chosen Latin names.

Arbor vitae
Tree of life
Finland

Conspectu mortis
In the view of death
Italy

Exitus letalis
A fatal exit
Russia

Honos aquilae
The honour of an eagle
France

Obscura nox hibernis
The dark winter's night
Italy

Pax mortis
The peace of death
United States

Silentium est aureum
Silence is golden
Germany

Ubique
Everywhere

This is the motto of the Corps of Royal Engineers and of the Royal Regiment of Artillery.

Ultimatum
A final warning

One of the best known of these is the ultimatum given by Britain to Germany to withdraw from Poland in 1939, her refusal to do so leading to the Second World War.

Ultra
Beyond

Outside the visible spectrum of light, the infra-red rays run in one direction and the ultra-violet in the other. 'Ultrasound' is sound beyond the normal range of human hearing.

Ultra vires
Beyond one's powers

Most organisations, committees and courts of law have a constitution, written or otherwise, which defines their duties and the power they have to see that their decisions are acted on. If they attempt to do anything which is beyond this agreed power, they are acting *ultra vires* and can be called to account for their excess enthusiasm.

Vale
Farewell

Veni, vidi vici
I came, I saw, I conquered

Julius Caesar, writing to Amantius, thus announces his victory over Pharnaces II at Zela in Pontus, in 47 BC.

Lawrence Durrell, in *Sauve Qui Peut*, 'What-ho on the Rialto', describes a French lady ambassador who wrought havoc with men's hearts in the Vulgarian diplomatic community, 'enmeshing them with her veni vidi vici' and whose tactics included 'tapping you on the lips with her closed fan'.

Verbatim
Word for word

In *Tom Jones*, Henry Fielding offers to present to the reader the text of a letter *verbatim et litteratim,* that is, not only word for word but letter for letter also, his reason for doing so becoming apparent immediately: 'Sir, I shud sartenly haf kaled you a cordin too mi promiss... '

Verbum sapienti sat est
A word to the wise is enough

Usually abbreviated to *verbum sap.* or even *verb. sap.*

> '*Verb. Sap.* Take the hint from me... Drop the
> monocle... Be a boozer... much more fun.'
>
> Aldous Huxley, 'The Monocle'

Versus (v. or vs.)
Against

Literally 'towards'. Any contest between two
opponents can be described as A *versus* B, e.g.
'Wolves v. Aston Villa'.

Veto

I forbid

The use of 'the veto' dates at least from Roman times. Except in procedural matters, each of the five permanent members of the United Nations Security Council – Britain, China, France, Russia and the United States – can use its veto to block any proposal supported by the other members of the Council. In the Cold War it was most frequently used by Russia to frustrate the aims of the United States and *vice versa*.

Via

By way of

The word *via* was Latin for a road or a way, as in *Via Dolorosa* ('the way of sorrows') and *Via Appia*, the Appian Way. However, the ablative form of *via* is also *via* and it is this latter which has the meaning 'by way of'. It may be used in a physical sense, as when a signpost points to 'Lamorna via Castallack', or in a non-physical sense, as when British Telecom states, 'You may use your BT Chargecard to dial via 144 from here'.

Vice

In place of

'Vice' is the ablative case of a noun whose nominative is not used. It appears frequently as a prefix – 'vice-captain', 'Vice-Chancellor', 'vice-chairman', 'viceroy' – and less frequently independently.

> 'The new man – *vice* Jollifant – certainly sounds a shrimp.'
>
> J. B. Priestley, *The Good Companions*

Vice versa

The other way around

Literally 'with the position turned'. It is a means of economising in words, so that 'Emily had great respect for George and George had great respect for Emily' can be reduced to 'Emily had great respect for George and vice versa'.

F. Anstey wrote a classic book called *Vice Versa* in which the persona of a boy migrated into the body of his father and, well, vice versa. It was made into a film in 1988.

Vide

See

An invitation to look at something, widely used in the present opus.

Videlicet (viz)

Namely

This is a contraction of the phrase *videre licet* ('one can see' or 'it is permitted to see'). A cursive 'z' was a common mark of contraction, particularly for –et, in medieval documents and inscriptions. At some point in the distant past the meaning mutated from 'one may see' to something like 'one may say', and this is its present meaning.

'… it is only possible for him to generate pleasure by the one means, *videlicet*, by screwing.'

Philip Larkin, 'Round Another Point'

Vim
Force, elbow grease

The O.E.D. suggests that 'vim' may possibly be the accusative case of *vis*, the Latin for 'force', used as the object of the verb in 'Use some blooming *vim*'.

Vis itself was used in the name 'Hōvis', where the little line over the 'o' had always puzzled me. The story goes that Hōvis is a contraction of *Hominum vis* ('the strength of men'), where *hō* is an accepted abbreviation of *hominum*.

Viva voce
With living voice

An oral examination. The phrase may also be used to imply reading aloud.

Viz
Videlicet, namely

vide videlicet

Vox humana
The human voice

The name given to a stop on an organ which has a wailing quality. It is mentioned in John Betjeman's poem 'In Westminster Abbey':

'Let me take this other glove off
As the *vox humana* swells… '

J. B. Priestley in *The Good Companions* gives us a picture of a cinema whose organ was no more than one 'relentless, quavering *vox humana* stop, and listening to it was like being forcibly fed by treacle'.

Vox Populi, vox Dei
The voice of the People is the voice of God

When he wrote this, Archbishop W. Reynolds was quoting Alcuin who used the expression in AD 800 but in a very negative context: 'We would not listen to those who say *"Vox Populi, vox Dei"*, for the voice of the people is near akin to madness.'

Vox populi when abbreviated to 'vox pop' refers to an extract from an interview with a member of the general public.

Acknowledgements

I should like to thank Dr Peter Jones of Friends of Classics and Dr Jenny March of the Classical Association for accepting articles for publication in their journals and so encouraging me (not a classicist by training), to compile the present book. I am greatly indebted to Mr Andrew Lownie for his support and encouragement in the writing of the book, and to Mr James Cochrane, who has offered invaluable help and advice in correcting and improving the text. I am also grateful to the publishers, Summersdale, for their help.

I must also thank Pan Macmillan and Mr Colin Dexter for their kind permission to reproduce extracts from Mr Dexter's books.

Other books from Summersdale

21st CENTURY LATIN

From ASBO Teens to Being Green

Sam Foster

21ST CENTURY LATIN

From ASBO Teens to Being Green

Sam Foster

ISBN: 978 84024 616 2   Hardback   £9.99

I'm really sorry, I sold your wife on eBay.

Me valde paenitet, sed vendidi mulierem tuam in eBay.

Am I bovvered?

Sollicitusne sum?

Hail, my fellow Latin-loving friends! No longer 'the dead language', Latin has been given a whole new lease of life for every situation we 21st-century folk find ourselves in.

If Latin's good enough for Caesar, it's good enough for you. And some things just sound far better in the old tongue.

From satnav and MySpace, to plastic surgery, organic gardening and online flirting, this Latin lover's phrase book will help you navigate modern life gracefully.

peculiar proverbs

weird words of wisdom from around the world.

stephen arnott

PECULIAR PROVERBS

Weird Words of Wisdom From Around the World

Stephen Arnott

ISBN: 978 84024 619 3   Hardback   £9.99

'*With patience and saliva, the ant swallows the elephant.*'
COLUMBIAN

'*Never bolt your door with a boiled carrot.*'
IRISH

This collection of genuine proverbs from cultures around the world ignores the common sayings we all know and concentrates on the unusual. Some are deft, witty and colourful, others plain weird. But they're all fascinating. With topics such as Wisdom and Discretion, Law and Order, Work (and Reasons Not To) and Love and Marriage, these quirky sayings provide much food for thought about human nature.

Peculiar Proverbs includes sayings you won't find in any other collection, sometimes so surreal they defy you to decipher them, providing hours of entertainment. Remember: *The man who tickles himself can laugh when he chooses.*

www.summersdale.com